Succeed in
Maths

Published by
Arcturus Publishing Limited
for Bookmart Limited
Registered Number 2372865
Trading as Bookmart Limited
Desford Road
Enderby
Leicester
LE19 4AD

This edition published 2002

ISBN 1-84193-079-2

Printed and bound in China

Author: Arthur Farndell
Consultant: Jenny Riley
Editor: Anne Fennell
Designer: Tania Field
Cover designer: Susi Martin

Succeed in Maths

A simple and clear guide to understanding the principles of Mathematics.

Key Stage 2 upper

Ages 9 to 11 years

Arthur Farndell

Consultant: Jenny Riley

Capella

Introduction

Succeed in Maths is an invaluable guide and exercise book for both parents and teachers wishing to guide children through the enjoyable although often problematic area of mathematics.

By the end of Key Stage 2 children should be able to handle numbers with ease; tackle fractions; decimals and percentages; understand and be able to put data into charts and graphs; have a grounding in geometry, and understand measures.

This book looks carefully at these main topics of the National Curriculum from a basic to a high level. Any topic which is deemed difficult is marked with a star. Those children who wish to be stretched to reach a high level of Key Stage 2 can have a go. The book is laid out so that a parent or teacher can help a child read through and understand the principles and methods of one topic on one page, while on the opposite page are exercises to test the child's understanding of these. The book has been designed so that most of the answers and workings out can be written straight onto the page. However there are occasions, including the grand revision test at the end of the book where your child will need a working notebook. For the geometry section a protractor, ruler and compass is required. Marks are awarded and the child can award him/herself a star if the whole page is correct.

Your child can work through this book at his/her own speed.
A topic a day can be taken, or more if the child has the energy.

Within a short period of time you should find that your child's understanding, speed and accuracy will improve and his/her marks will get better.

Good luck and good practising!

Contents

units, tens and hundreds

It is an amazing fact that with just 9 digits and *zero we can perform all mathematical calculations*. The 10 symbols are so simple and yet so powerful. This is why we need to understand the laws under which they operate.

Place value

The first law is the law of **place value**. This means that the value of a digit (*figure*) is governed by its **place** in a number.

In these examples look at the position of 1 to see its place value.

TTh	Th	H	T	U	
				1	the **1** by itself has the value of **one unit = 1**.
			1	2	the **1** has the value of **one ten = 10**.
		1	2	3	the **1** has the value of **one hundred = 100**.
	1	2	3	4	the **1** has the value of **one thousand = 1000**.
1	2	3	4	5	the **1** has the value of **ten thousand = 10,000**.

Rounding numbers

Rounding numbers is not a law, but a rule. This means expressing a number **approximately** rather than precisely. You might say that 50,000 people attended a football match. It is not completely accurate but it gives an idea of how many people were there. The number is **rounded** to the nearest thousand.

Method: You are asked to express 86 to the nearest **ten**. Look at the last digit of 86. Because the last digit is in the range 5 – 9 you go upwards, and the answer is 90. (90 is called a **ten** because it is in the ten times table).

With 84 you go downwards, and the answer is 80.

You might be asked to express 86 to the nearest **hundred**. Because 86 is in the range 50 – 99 the answer is 100.

Study these examples to make sure you understand:

43	rounded to the nearest	**10**	is	**40**.
123	rounded to the nearest	**10**	is	**120**.
123	rounded to the nearest	**100**	is	**100**.
2,936	rounded to the nearest	**1,000**	is	**3,000**.

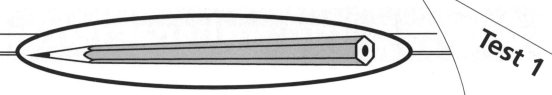

Place Value

In the boxes write the different values of 2 and 5, and of 1 and 4.

	T/Th.	Th.	H	T	U	Value of 2	Value of 5
a.			2	3	5	200	5
b.		2	4	5	7		
c.			5	9	2		
d.	2	5	3	0	8		
e.	5	9	0	2	3		
						Value of 1	Value of 4
f.	1	9	4	2	3		
g.		4	0	1	3		
h.			6	4	1		
i.	5	8	1	2	4		

Rounding

j. 29 rounded to the nearest 10 is _____

k. 75 rounded to the nearest 10 is _____

l. 75 rounded to the nearest 100 is _____

m. 268 rounded to the nearest 100 is _____

n. 3704 rounded to the nearest 1,000 is _____

o. round 23 to the nearest 10 _____

p. round 27 to the nearest 10 _____

q. round 349 to the nearest 100 _____

r. round 6,231 to the nearest 1,000 _____

s. round 74 to the nearest 10 _____

Mark your score out of 19:

_____
19

If you have got all the questions correct, colour in this star.

7

Adding and subtracting

On pages 4 and 5 we saw the importance of **place value**.
Place value *plays a vital part in all addition and subtraction.*

Let us take **addition** first.

Adding

Addition

Suppose you have **3 0 2 + 2 1 3 + 4 6 8 5 + 1 4**.

If you **ignore** place value and write the addition like this:

```
    3   0   2
    2   1   3
    4   6   8   5
+   1   4
---------------------
```

your answer will be wrong!
1. Instead, set it out by giving
each digit its correct **place value**:

Th	H	T	U
	3	0	2
	2	1	3
4	6	8	5
+		1	4
5	**2**	**1**	**4**
	1	*1*	*1*

2. Add all the units (=14).
Write 4 in the units column and carry 1.
Add the tens (=10 +1 carried over =11).
Write 1 and carry 1.
3. Add the hundreds (=11+1 carried
over = 12). Write 2 and carry 1.
4. Add the thousands (=4+1 carried
over +5). Write 5.

Subtracting

Subtraction

Suppose you have **361 – 34**. Set the work out according
to **place value**.

H	T	U
3	^{5}6	^{1}1
–		3	4
3	**2**	**7**

1. Now look at the units.
You cannot take 4 from 1.
Borrow one of the tens, so that you
now have **11 units** and **5 tens**.

2. Take 4 from 11 (=7).

3. Look at the tens. You can take
3 from 5: 5–3 = 2

4. Look at the hundreds. 3 take
away nothing is 3. The answer is 327.

Addition

a. 213 + 46 + 62 + 545
b. 372 + 891 + 1070 + 19
c. 28 + 34 + 127 + 2305

> **Tip.** *If you have to add money or metres or kilograms or centimetres, just follow the same process.*

Set your work out according to **place value**.

a. Th H T U   **b.** Th H T U   **c.** Th H T U

+
-----------------   +
-----------------   +
----

ans
-----------------   -----------------   -----------------

Subtraction

d.
```
      2  3
  -   2  3
-----------------

-----------------
```

e.
```
      9  8
  -   6  6
-----------------

-----------------
```

f.
```
      9  0  7
  -      9  6
-----------------

-----------------
```

g.
```
      5  0  9
  -      7  1
-----------------

-----------------
```

h.
```
      2  8  4
  -      7  6
-----------------

-----------------
```

i.
```
      2  8  5
  -      1  8
-----------------

-----------------
```

j.
```
  £   9  .  9  2
  -   4  .  1  0
-----------------
  £
-----------------
```

k.
```
      3  7  3  m
  -      9  8  m
-----------------
            m
-----------------
```

l.
```
      3  4  8
  -   1  2  5
-----------------

-----------------
```

Mark your score out of 12:

___
12

If you have got all the questions correct, colour in this star.

9

long multiplication

Long multiplication involves numbers of two or more digits.
To do the work correctly you need three things:
1. A knowledge of your **tables,** up to the 9 times table.
2. An understanding of **place value** (*see page 4*).
3. A **method**.

Method: *e.g. 372 x 18*

(see page 4)

Step 1

Th	H	T	U
	3	7	2
x		1	8

Set out the work according to **place value**.

Step 2

Multiply 372 by 8 units, remembering to carry figures where necessary.

Th	H	T	U
	3	7	2
x		1	8

2	9	7	6
	5	1	

1. 8 x 2 = 16. Write 6 in the units and carry 1.
2. 8 x 7 = 56. 56 + 1 = 57. Write 7 in the tens and carry 5.
3. 8 x 3 = 24. 24 + 5 = 29. Write 9 in the hundreds and 2 in the thousands.
So, 372 x 8 = 2976

Step 3

Multiply 372 by 1 ten.

Th	H	T	U
	3	7	2
x		1	8

2	9	7	6
3	7	2	0

Because you are now multiplying by the tens column, put zero in the units column.
1 x 2 = 2. Write 2 in the tens.
1 x 7 = 7. Write 7 in the hundreds.
1 x 3 = 3. Write 3 in the thousands.
So, 372 x 10 = 3720.

Step 4

Add the two answers to obtain the final answer.

Th	H	T	U
	3	7	2
x		1	8

2	9	7	6
3	7	2	0

6	6	9	6

This is 372 x 8 units.
This is 372 x 1 ten.

This is 372 x 18.

Tip: *Any number multiplied by zero is zero.*

Now use your knowledge of the tables, your understanding of place value and the method given on page 8 to do this:

a.

Th	H	T	U
	2	1	6
x		1	4

----

b.

Th	H	T	U
		9	7
x		7	2

----

c.

Th	H	T	U
		1	4	5
x			2	6

----

d.

Th	H	T	U
	3	0	8
x		1	3

----

e.

Th	H	T	U
	1	9	0
x		3	1

----

f.

Th	H	T	U
		8	6
x		9	8

----

g.

Th	H	T	U
	1	1	3
x		2	1

----

h.

Th	H	T	U
		7	2
x		8	4

----

i.

Th	H	T	U
	2	1	5
x		1	8

----

j.   There are 26 T-shirts in a box.
How many are there in 15 boxes?

k.   A baking tray holds 18 cakes,
How many cakes do 17 trays hold?

long division

If you were asked to divide 20 by 5, you could probably give the answer immediately; 4. But some division work is too hard for most of us to do in our heads. This is called **Long Division**. To do **Long Division** properly you need:

1. An understanding of **place value** (see page 4)

> **Remainder**

2. An understanding that there may be a **remainder.**
   A remainder is produced when a number does not divide exactly into another number. *For example: 21 ÷ 4: -
   4 does not divide into 21 exactly; it divides 5 times with 1 left over. This left over number is called the* **remainder**.
3. A **method**.

Method

Now move to the method to solve 4,926 ÷ 16

> **Step 1**

Set the work out, showing the **place values** for 4,926

	Th	H	T	U
16	4	9	2	6

> **Step 2**

	Th	H	T	U
		3		
16	4	9	2	6
	4	8		
		1		

How many 16s in 4? None.
Leave a blank in the thousands.

How many 16s in 49?
3. Write 3 in the hundreds.
16 x 3 = 48. Write 48 beneath 49.
Subtract, to get remainder 1.

> **Step 3**

	Th	H	T	U
		3	0	
16	4	9	2	6
	4	8		
		1	2	

Bring down the 2.
How many 16s in 12? None.
Write zero in the tens.

> **Step 4**

	Th	H	T	U
		3	0	7
16	4	9	2	6
	4	8		
		1	2	6
		1	1	2
			1	4

Bring down the 6 in the units column to make 126.

How many 16s in 126?
16 x 6 is 96 (*too small*)
and 16 x 8 is 128 (*too big*).
16 x 7 is 112. Write 7 in the units column and write 112 beneath 126 and subtract. This gives 14, which is smaller than 16. The remainder is 14.
The final answer is 307 r.14.

Tip:
Use multiplication grid at the back of the book to help you.

12

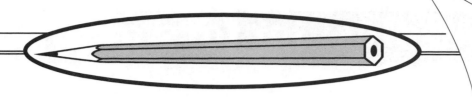

> **Tip:** Use the grid at the back of the book to help you with difficult numbers.
> Alternatively write the x table of the divisor to help you,
> e.g. for the sum 4926 ÷ 16 you might write out the 16 x table.

a.   H T U

12 | 2 9 2

b.   H T U

13 | 7 9 4

c.   H T U

14 | 9 3 5

d.   Th H T U

15 | 6 7 0 2

e.   Th H T U

16 | 9 2 4 3

f.   Th H T U

17 | 1 8 9 6

g.   Th H T U

18 | 3 6 5 4

h.   Th H T U

19 | 5 7 9 7

i.   Th H T U

20 | 4 0 0 0

j.   A local charity donated 1426 books to be shared
equally among 18 schools.
How many books did each school receive?

k.   When the old man died, half of his money went
to his wife, and the remainder was shared equally
by his 14 surviving relatives. He left £51,464.
How much did each of the 14 relatives receive?

Mark
your score
out of II:

⎯⎯

II

If you have
got all the
questions
correct,
colour in
this star.

13

multiples, factors and primes

Multiple

A **multiple** *is the result of multiplying one number by another.*

3 x 2 = 6.   *So* 6 is a multiple of 3.
6 is also a multiple of 2.

All the answers in the 3 times table are multiples of 3:
3, 6, 9, 12, 15, 18, 21, 24, 27, 30, 33, 36.

All the answers in the 7 times table are multiples of 7:
7, 14, 21, 28, 35, 42, 49, 56, 63, 70, 77, 84.

Factor

A **factor** *is a number that divides exactly (with no remainder) into another number.*

5 is a **factor** of **15**. (5 x 3 = 15)

3 is also a **factor** of **15**.

1 is a **factor** of **15**,
because 1 is a factor of every number.

15 is a **factor** of **15**,
since every number divides into itself exactly once.

15 *therefore has* **4 factors**: **1, 3, 5, 15.**

12, *though smaller, has* **6 factors**: **1, 2, 3, 4, 6, 12.**

Prime

A **prime** *is a number that has only 2 factors: 1 and the number itself.*

The first three **prime numbers** are **2, 3, 5**.
(*1 is not included, because* **1** *has only* **one** *factor!*)

Prime factor

A **prime factor** *is a prime number that divides exactly into another number.*

Thus, as we have seen, the **factors** of **15** are **1, 3, 5,** and **15**.
But: the **prime factors** of **15** are **3** and **5** only.

Multiples

Continue the sequence.

a. | 6 | 12 | ☐ | ☐ | ☐ | ☐ | ☐

b. | 7 | 14 | ☐ | ☐ | ☐ | ☐ | ☐

c. | 8 | 16 | ☐ | ☐ | ☐ | ☐ | ☐

d. | 9 | 18 | ☐ | ☐ | ☐ | ☐ | ☐

e. | 12 | 24 | ☐ | ☐ | ☐ | ☐ | ☐

Factors

Complete **f.** to **j**. Write the factors in order, beginning with the smallest.

f. The factors of 6 are ☐ ☐ ☐ ☐

g. The factors of 8 are ☐ ☐ ☐ ☐

h. The factors of 16 are ☐ ☐ ☐ ☐ ☐

i. The factors of 20 are ☐ ☐ ☐ ☐ ☐ ☐

j. The factors of 30 are ☐ ☐ ☐ ☐ ☐ ☐ ☐ ☐

Primes

Continue this list of prime numbers.

k. | 2 | 3 | ☐ | ☐ | ☐ | ☐ | ☐

Prime factors

Complete **l.** and **m.** Write the prime factors in order, beginning with the smallest.

l. The prime factors of 6 are ☐ ☐

m. The prime factors of 30 are ☐ ☐ ☐

Mark your score out of 13:

_____

13

If you have got all the questions correct, colour in this star.

15

fractions ⭐ HIGH

Fraction

A **fraction** *is a part of something.*
The most common fraction is a **half**, which is 1 of 2 equal parts and can be written as $\frac{1}{2}$.

The top number of a fraction is the **numerator**,
and the lower number is the **denominator**.

Other fractions

$\frac{1}{3}$ $\frac{1}{3}$ = (one third) is 1 of 3 equal parts that make one whole.

$\frac{2}{3}$ $\frac{2}{3}$ = (two thirds) is 2 of 3 equal parts that make one whole.

$\frac{1}{4}$ $\frac{3}{4}$ $\frac{4}{4}$ $\frac{2}{5}$

(one quarter)   (three quarters)   (four quarters or one whole)   there are 5 parts in all, 2 are shaded (two fifths)

Equivalent fraction

If a whole pizza was divided into 4 equal pieces and someone took 2 pieces, we could say that they had taken half of the pizza.

Another way of saying this, would be that they had taken $\frac{2}{4}$. A $\frac{1}{2}$ is the same as $\frac{2}{4}$.

Likewise

$\frac{2}{3}$ = $\frac{4}{6}$

Cancelling fractions

This means *dividing the numerator and the denominator by their highest common factor* (**HCF**), the highest number that goes into both.

In $\frac{4}{6}$, 2 is the HCF. $4 \div 2 = 2$, $6 \div 2 = 3$.

Thus, to cancel $\frac{4}{6}$ we write $\frac{4^2}{6^3}$ = $\frac{2}{3}$.

What fraction is shaded ?

a.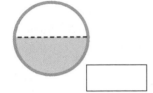

b.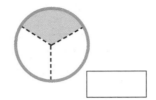

c.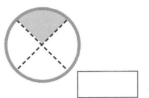

d.

e.

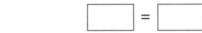

f.

g.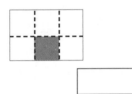

h.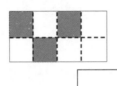

i.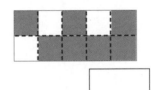

Cancel these fractions. Remember to divide the numerator and the denominator by the highest number that goes into both.

j. $\frac{4}{6}$ =

k. $\frac{2}{4}$ =

l. $\frac{2}{6}$ =

m. $\frac{3}{6}$ =

n. $\frac{4}{8}$ =

o. $\frac{2}{8}$ =

p. $\frac{3}{9}$ =

q. $\frac{2}{10}$ =

r. $\frac{5}{10}$ =

s. $\frac{4}{10}$ =

t. $\frac{6}{10}$ =

u. $\frac{8}{10}$ =

v. $\frac{2}{12}$ =

w. $\frac{3}{12}$ =

x. $\frac{4}{12}$ =

y. $\frac{6}{9}$ =

z. $\frac{9}{12}$ =

In any fraction the **numerator** (*top number*) and the **denominator** (*lower number*) are equally important in telling us how big the fraction is.

When we want to *add two or more fractions which have the same denominator, we simply add the numerators together but keep the same denominator*.

For example: $\frac{2}{9} + \frac{5}{9} = \frac{7}{9}$ and $\frac{1}{11} + \frac{2}{11} + \frac{3}{11} = \frac{6}{11}$

The same is true of **subtracting** fractions with the same denominator. *Thus:* $\frac{5}{9} - \frac{1}{9} = \frac{4}{9}$

Adding fractions with different denominators

For example: $\frac{1}{2} + \frac{1}{3}$

Step 1 Find the lowest number that 2 and 3 both divide into exactly. This is **6**.
This number is called the **Lowest Common Denominator** (LCD).

Step 2 Take the first fraction ($\frac{1}{2}$).
Divide the LCD (**6**) by the *denominator* (**2**) and multiply the answer by the *numerator* (**1**):
$6 \div 2 = 3$, $3 \times 1 = 3$.
This gives **3** as the *new numerator*. We can express $\frac{1}{2}$ as $\frac{3}{6}$.

Step 3 In the same way we can express the second fraction ($\frac{1}{3}$) as $\frac{2}{6}$.

Step 4 Now that our two fractions have the *same denominator* (**6**), we can *add the two numerators* to give the final answer:

The full working is: $\frac{1}{2} + \frac{1}{3} = \frac{3}{6} + \frac{2}{6} = \frac{5}{6}$

Use the same method when subtracting fractions with different denominators.

Thus: $\frac{1}{2} - \frac{1}{3} = \frac{3}{6} - \frac{2}{6} = \frac{1}{6}$

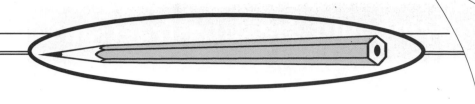

Adding fractions with the same denominator.

a. $\frac{1}{9} + \frac{4}{9} = \boxed{}$

b. $\frac{1}{5} + \frac{3}{5} = \boxed{}$

c. $\frac{1}{3} + \frac{1}{3} = \boxed{}$

d. $\frac{4}{7} + \frac{2}{7} = \boxed{}$

e. $\frac{1}{8} + \frac{1}{8} + \frac{5}{8} = \boxed{}$

f. $\frac{1}{10} + \frac{3}{10} + \frac{3}{10} = \boxed{}$

g. $\frac{1}{9} + \frac{3}{9} = \boxed{}$

h. $\frac{2}{11} + \frac{3}{11} + \frac{5}{11} = \boxed{}$

i. $\frac{1}{12} + \frac{5}{12} + \frac{5}{12} = \boxed{}$

Subtracting fractions with the same denominator.

j. $\frac{4}{5} - \frac{1}{5} = \boxed{}$

k. $\frac{2}{3} - \frac{1}{3} = \boxed{}$

l. $\frac{5}{7} - \frac{2}{7} = \boxed{}$

m. $\frac{6}{11} - \frac{2}{11} = \boxed{}$

n. $\frac{16}{17} - \frac{9}{17} = \boxed{}$

o. $\frac{19}{23} - \frac{7}{23} = \boxed{}$

p. $\frac{7}{19} - \frac{2}{19} = \boxed{}$

q. $\frac{17}{21} - \frac{9}{21} = \boxed{}$

r. $\frac{8}{15} - \frac{6}{15} = \boxed{}$

Adding fractions with different denominators.

s. $\frac{1}{3} + \frac{1}{4} = \frac{}{12} + \frac{}{12} = \frac{}{12}$

t. $\frac{1}{4} + \frac{1}{5} = \frac{}{20} + \frac{}{20} = \frac{}{20}$

u. $\frac{1}{2} + \frac{1}{4} = \boxed{} = \boxed{}$

v. $\frac{3}{10} + \frac{1}{5} = \boxed{} = \boxed{} = \boxed{}$ *

w. $\frac{1}{3} + \frac{1}{6} = \boxed{} = \boxed{} = \boxed{}$ *

x. $\frac{1}{3} + \frac{1}{7} = \boxed{} = \boxed{}$

Subtracting fractions with different denominators.

y. $\frac{2}{9} - \frac{3}{18} = \boxed{} = \boxed{}$

z. $\frac{5}{6} - \frac{3}{18} = \boxed{} = \boxed{} = \boxed{}$ *

aa. $\frac{3}{4} - \frac{5}{8} = \boxed{} = \boxed{}$

bb. $\frac{5}{7} - \frac{6}{21} = \boxed{} = \boxed{} = \boxed{}$ *

* *Cancel*

Mark your score out of 28:

$\dfrac{}{28}$

If you have got all the questions correct, colour in this star.

19

multiplying and dividing fractions

Multiplying

When we want to **multiply two fractions**,
1. we *multiply the two numerators* (*top numbers*)
2. *then the two denominators* (bottom *numbers*).

1st example: $\frac{1}{4} \times \frac{1}{5} = \frac{1}{20}$

Cancelling fractions

2nd example: $\frac{2}{5} \times \frac{1}{2}$

1. We can cancel across the multiplication.

> *Tip. A **whole number** is a simple number without any fractions: eg. 1,2,3.*
>
> *A **mixed number** is a whole number together with a fraction:*
>
> *e.g.* $1\frac{1}{2}$, $2\frac{1}{4}$, $3\frac{1}{2}$.

$\frac{1}{5}^{^1}\!\!2 \times \frac{1}{2}^{^1}$

2. The numerator 2 & the denominator 2 have an HCF that both go into, which is 2.
(For HCF see page 16)

$\frac{1}{5} \times \frac{1}{1} = \frac{1}{5}$

3. Multiply as before.

3rd example: $\frac{8}{9} \times \frac{3}{4}$

Here there are two HCFs.
The HCF of **8** and **4** is **4**, so we divide 8 and 4 by 4,
and the HCF of **3** and **9** is *3*,
so we divide **9** and **3** by **3**.

${}^2\frac{8}{9}_3 \times {}^1\frac{3}{4}_1 = \frac{2}{3}$

Dividing

When we want to **divide one fraction by another**, we *turn the second fraction* (*the divisor*), **upside down** and we *change the division sign to a multiplication sign*. Then we proceed exactly as we do when multiplying.

> *Tip. A **top heavy fraction** is a fraction where the top number (numerator) is bigger than the lower number (denominator):*
>
> *e.g.* $\frac{3}{2}$, $\frac{4}{3}$, $\frac{4}{3}$.

1st example: $\frac{1}{9} \div \frac{1}{4} = \frac{1}{9} \times \frac{4}{1} = \frac{4}{9}$

2nd example: $\frac{5}{18} \div \frac{2}{9} = \frac{5}{{}_2 18} \times \frac{9^{^1}}{2} = \frac{5}{4}$

Our answer is **top-heavy** at present, because the numerator is bigger than the denominator (5 is bigger than 4).
Let us change it to a **mixed number** by *dividing the denominator into the numerator*, to obtain **1 r 1**
(5 goes into 4 once with 1 over).
This remainder means *1 over 4* or $\frac{1}{4}$.

So the final answer is: $1\frac{1}{4}$

The full working is: $\frac{5}{18} \div \frac{2}{9} = \frac{5}{{}_2 18} \times \frac{9^{^1}}{2} = \frac{5}{4} = 1\frac{1}{4}$

Multiplying. * *Cancel*

a. $\frac{1}{9} \times \frac{2}{3}$ = ☐

b. $\frac{1}{10} \times \frac{3}{5}$ = ☐

c. $\frac{1}{2} \times \frac{1}{3}$ = ☐

d. $\frac{1}{2} \times \frac{1}{2}$ = ☐

e. $\frac{1}{2} \times \frac{1}{4}$ = ☐

f. $\frac{1}{4} \times \frac{1}{4}$ = ☐

g. $\frac{1}{3} \times \frac{2}{5}$ = ☐

h. $\frac{3}{7} \times \frac{1}{2}$ = ☐

i. $\frac{3}{8} \times \frac{2}{3}$ = ☐ *

j. $\frac{4}{9} \times \frac{3}{8}$ = ☐ *

k. $\frac{2}{5} \times \frac{10}{11}$ = ☐ *

l. $\frac{5}{6} \times \frac{7}{10}$ = ☐ *

Change these top heavy fractions into mixed numbers:

m. $\frac{5}{4}$ = ☐

n. $\frac{9}{5}$ = ☐

o. $\frac{3}{2}$ = ☐

p. $\frac{11}{9}$ = ☐

q. $\frac{13}{7}$ = ☐

r. $\frac{15}{6}$ = ☐ = ☐ *

Dividing.

s. $\frac{1}{8} \div \frac{2}{3}$ = ☐ = ☐

t. $\frac{2}{7} \div \frac{3}{5}$ = ☐ = ☐

u. $\frac{4}{9} \div \frac{1}{3}$ = ☐ = ☐ = ☐ *

v. $\frac{3}{4} \div \frac{1}{8}$ = ☐ = ☐ *

w. $\frac{3}{8} \div \frac{2}{3}$ = ☐ = ☐

x. $\frac{4}{5} \div \frac{2}{15}$ = ☐ = ☐ *

y. $\frac{2}{9} \div \frac{3}{9}$ = ☐ = ☐ *

z. $\frac{5}{11} \div \frac{10}{33}$ = ☐ = ☐ = ☐ *

aa. $\frac{1}{4} \div \frac{1}{2}$ = ☐ = ☐ *

bb. $\frac{1}{3} \div \frac{1}{6}$ = ☐ = ☐ *

cc. $\frac{1}{6} \div \frac{1}{3}$ = ☐ = ☐ *

dd. $\frac{7}{10} \div \frac{1}{5}$ = ☐ = ☐ = ☐ *

Mark your score out of 30:

$\frac{\qquad}{30}$

If you have got all the questions correct, colour in this star.

decimals

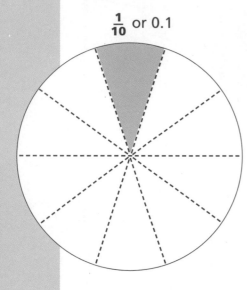

$\frac{1}{10}$ or 0.1

A **decimal** *is also a* **part** *of something*.
We start by looking at **tenths**. When a pizza is cut into 10 equal parts, each part is a **tenth**. *The decimal form for a tenth is 0.1* (nought point one).

For *2 tenths we write 0.2* (nought point two).
For *3 tenths we have 0.3*, for *four tenths 0.4* and so on.

Decimals also take account of **hundredths**.
If something is cut into 100 equal pieces,
each part is a **hundredth**.
The decimal for a hundredth is 0.01 (nought point nought one).
For *2 hundredths we write 0.02* (nought point nought two).

The law of **place value** operates here too.
Just as we have **Th H T U** for whole numbers, so for decimals we have *Tenths, Hundredths* and *Thousandths*.

Here is the scheme for whole numbers and decimals:

Th	H	T	U	decimal point	tenths	hundredths	thousandths
1	2	3	4	.	5	6	7

Adding

The vital thing **when adding decimals** is to *keep everything, including the decimal point, in the right columns according to the law of* **place value**. The rest is normal addition.
First example: 0.27 + 0.47

Units	decimal point	Tenths	Hundredths	Thousandths
0	.	2	7	
+ 0	.	4	7	
0	.	7	4	

1

Answer: **0.74**

Subtracting

Keep everything in the right columns. Borrow if necessary.
First example: 0.835 - 0.679

Units	decimal point	Tenths	Hundredths	Thousandths
0	.	7 8̶	12 3̶	1 5
- 0	.	6	7	9
0	.	1	5	6

Answer: **0.156**

Adding

a. 0 . 5 6
   + 0 . 4 7

   ----

b. 0 . 0 4 1
   + 0 . 7 6 8

   ----

c. 1 . 2
   + 3 . 4 8 9

   ----

d. 4 9 . 1 0 2
   + 0 . 0 1 7

   ----

e. 2 1 . 6 7
   + 3 . 2 9

   ----

f. 0 . 0 5 4
   + 1 . 2 4 8

   ----

g. 2 . 4 5 9
   + 0 . 0 6

   ----

h. 0 . 0 0 2
   + 0 . 0 2 5

   ----

i. 6 . 0 2
   + 1 . 4 5

   ----

j. 2 . 3 8 1
   + 1 . 7 4 3

   ----

k. 0 . 7 8 9
   + 0 . 1 2 3

   ----

l. 3 . 0 0 7
   + 2 . 7 0 7

Subtracting

m. 0 . 9 8
   − 0 . 2 5

   ----

n. 0 . 5 4
   − 0 . 0 9

   ----

o. 0 . 7 6
   − 0 . 5 9 2

   ----

p. 0 . 7 6 8 5
   − 0 . 2 9 9 7

   ----

q. 0 . 9 4
   − 0 . 2 3

   ----

r. 0 . 5 1
   − 0 . 1 9

   ----

s. 1 . 8 5 4
   − 1 . 7 2 9

   ----

t. 2 . 3 0 4
   − 1 . 2 6 7

   ----

u. 4 . 0 3
   − 3 . 7 2

   ----

v. 1 . 1 4
   − 0 . 0 9

   ----

w. 0 . 1 7 6
   − 0 . 0 5 4

   ----

x. 0 . 0 9 5
   − 0 . 0 7 9

Mark
your score
out of 24:

$$\frac{\quad}{24}$$

If you have
got all the
questions
correct,
colour in
this star.

23

decimals — multiplying and dividing by 10 & 100

Multiply by 10

Multiplying decimals by 10
Move the numbers one place to the left.

Examples:

H	T	U	.	t	h	th					H	T	U	.	t	h	th
		0	.	6	2	5	x	10	=				6	.	2	5	
		0	.	6	2		x	10	=				6	.	2		
		2	.	6			x	10	=			2	6				

Multiply by 100

Multiplying decimals by 100
Move the numbers two places to the left.

Examples:

H	T	U	.	t	h	th					H	T	U	.	t	h	th
		0	.	6	2	5	x	100	=			6	2	.	5		
		0	.	6	2		x	100	=			6	2				
		2	.	6			x	100	=	2	6	0					

Divide by 10

Dividing decimals by 10
Move the numbers one place to the right.

Examples:

H	T	U	.	t	h	th					H	T	U	.	t	h	th	tth
		0	.	6	2	5	÷	10	=				0	.	0	6	2	5
		1	.	2	3		÷	10	=				0	.	1	2	3	
	1	2	.	3			÷	10	=				1	.	2	3		

Divide by 100

Dividing decimals by 100
Move the numbers two places to the right.

Examples:

H	T	U	.	t	h	th					H	T	U	.	t	h	th	tth
		3	.	6	1		÷	100	=				0	.	0	3	6	1
	3	7	.	4			÷	100	=				0	.	3	7	4	
1	4	0	.	6			÷	100	=				1	.	4	0	6	

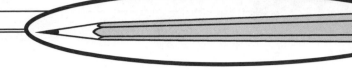

Multiplying by 10

a. 0.7 x 10 = [ ]

b. 0.68 x 10 = [ ]

c. 1.25 x 10 = [ ]

d. 0.01 x 10 = [ ]

Multiplying by 100

e. 0.428 x 100 = [ ]

f. 0.3 x 100 = [ ]

g. 6.502 x 100 = [ ]

h. 0.002 x 100 = [ ]

Dividing by 10

i. 0.7 ÷ 10 = [ ]

j. 0.05 ÷ 10 = [ ]

k. 1.2 ÷ 10 = [ ]

l. 24.67 ÷ 10 = [ ]

Dividing by 100

m. 16.76 ÷ 100 = [ ]

n. 2.65 ÷ 100 = [ ]

o. 179.8 ÷ 100 = [ ]

p. 3794.01 ÷ 100 = [ ]

Mark your score out of 16:

———
16

If you have got all the questions correct, colour in this star.

25

percentages

You remember that *a percentage is usually a part of something*.
One percent (**1%**) means a **one-hundredth part**.
2% means **two-hundredths**, and so on.

Sometimes you find **100% = the whole and not a part**,
as in '*100% Pure Orange Juice,*'
which means that nothing has been added to the juice.

In business life you can find percentages *higher than 100*!
For example, if you buy an item for £1000 and then sell it for
£3000, you have made a profit of £2000,
which is *twice as much as you paid* for the item.
This profit, being *twice the original cost*, can be described
as **200% profit**!

1st example: What is 3% of £100?
        Divide £100 by 100 (*£100 ÷ 100 = £1*).
        So   **1%** of £100 is **£1**
        Therefore **3%** = 3 x £1 = **£3**

2nd example: What is 50% of 20?
        Remember that 50% is a half.
        A **half of 20** is **10**

3rd example: What is 60% of 400?
        400 ÷ 100 = 4. So 4 is 1% of 400.
        To find **60%**, **multiply 4** by **60** (*= 240*).
        Therefore **60%** of 400 is **240**.

4th example: A suit was reduced by 10%.
The original price was £300. What was the reduced price?

        Find 10% of £300, like this: $\frac{300}{100}$ x **10** = £30

        Subtract £30 from the original price
        to find the reduced price:
        £300 – £30 = £270

5th example: There are 20 children on the class register.
Today 3 children are away. What percentage are present?

        First find the percentage absent.
        Multiply 3 by 100 and **divide by 20**: $3 \times \frac{\overset{5}{\cancel{100}}}{\underset{1}{\cancel{20}}} = 15$
        15% are **absent**,
    so **85%** are **present** (*15% + 85% = 100%*).

a. What is 5% of £100?

b. What is 50% of £60?
Tip: Remember 50% is a half.

c. What is 20% of £200?

d. What is 1% of £8?
Tip: First change £8 to pence.

e. What is 25% of 20m?
Tip: Remember that 25% is a quarter.

f. What is 10% of £1000?
Tip: 10% is a tenth.

g. A supermarket is reducing the price of its own brand washing powder by 10%. The original price is £2.50. What is the reduced price?

h. In the class there are 11 girls and 11 boys. What percentage of the class are boys?

i. John got two answers wrong in a test. There were 20 questions. What was his mark as a percentage?

j. There are 500 children in the school. Today 25 children are away, what percentage are present?

Mark your score out of 10:

_____
10

If you have got all the questions correct, colour in this star.

27

doubling and halving

Doubling *means multiplying by 2.*

Double 4 = 8

You have won £250. If you doubled your prize you would have *£500*.

Doubling twice — In this way you can see that *doubling and doubling again* is the same as *multiplying by 4*.
When the £250 prize money is doubled and doubled again, it becomes £1,000. This is the same as saying **£250 x 4 = £1,000**.

Doubling large numbers — For example, *we can remove the nought from 250 (as long as we remember to return it later!).*
Two 25s are **50**. Return the nought, and the *answer is* **500**.

If this, too, seems hard, you can say: Two 20s are 40 and *two 5s are ten.* So two *25s are 40 + 10, which is 50*.
Return the nought, and the *correct answer is still* **500**.
500 x 2 is even easier. This time you can remove both noughts, and you are left with **5**.
5 x 2 = 10. Return the two noughts, and the correct answer is **1,000**.

Halving *means dividing by 2.*

If there have been 600 criminal offences per month in a particular area, and the crime rate is then *halved*, it means that there are *now 300 offences every month*.
If this new rate is halved there will be only *150 offences* per month.

Halving twice — So *halving and halving again* is the same as *dividing by 4*.
Thus **600 ÷ 4 = 150**.

Here are some useful halves to know:
Half an hour = 30 minutes
Half a kilogram (kg) = 500 grammes (g)
Half a kilometre (km) = 500 metres (m)
Half a centimetre (cm) = 5 millimetres (mm)
Half of £1 = 50p
Half of £3 = £1.50
Half of £5 = £2.50
Half of 1000 = 500
Half of 500 = 250
Half of 250 = 125
Half of 125 = 62.5

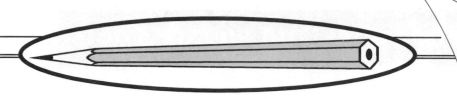

Doubling.

Continue this doubling sequence. Notice how it soon becomes very large.

a. | 1 | 2 | 4 | 8 | | | | | | | |

Now double these amounts.   See how many you can do in your head.

b. 25 _____ **c.** 35 _____ **d.** 45 _____ **e.** £1.50 _____

f. £2.25 _____ **g.** £1.15 _____ **h.** 150 _____ **i.** 450 _____

j. 650 _____ **k.** 75 _____ **l.** 175 _____ **m.** 275 _____

n. 2.5 _____ **o.** 9.5 _____ **p.** 12.5 _____ **q.** 5mm _____

r. 500m _____ **s.** 750g _____

Halving

Continue this halving sequence.

t. | 1200 | 600 | | | |

Now halve these amounts. Can you do them all in your head?

u. £8 _____ **v.** £7 _____ **w.** £15 _____ **x.** 50 _____

y. 70 _____ **z.** 90 _____ **aa.** 2 000 000 _____

bb. 1 000 000 _____ **cc.** 1kg _____ **dd.** 98m _____

ee. 3:2 _____

ff. In the village there are 2700 inhabitants.
50% are male. How many inhabitants are female? _____

Mark your score out of 32:

_____
32

If you have got all the questions correct, colour in this star.

29

squares, cubes and square roots

The square *of a number is the answer you obtain when you multiply that number by itself.*

So the *square of 2 = 2 x 2 = 4*.
4 is called a **square number** because it can be represented by *4 dots in the form of a square.*

Similarly, the *square of 3 = 3 x 3 = 9*.
9 dots can also form a square.

All the square numbers are like this.
A simple way to write the *square of 2* is 2^2 (*two squared*)
The *square of 3* is usually written as 3^2 (*three squared*), and so on.

The cube *of a number is the answer you obtain when you multiply the square of the number by itself.*

Thus the *cube of 2 = 4 x 2 = 8*.
What this shows is that the *cube of 2* is really **2 x 2 x 2 = 8**.

It is called a **cube** because
8 dots can show the shape of a cube.
A simple way to write the *cube of 2* is 2^3 (*two cubed*).

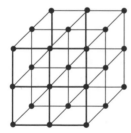

Likewise, the *cube of 3* is **3 x 3 x 3 = 27**.
This can be written as 3^3 (*three cubed*).
27 dots form this **cube**.

The square root *of a number is a number that when multiplied by itself gives the original number.*

4 is the square of 2, (2 x 2 = 4)
and so *2 is called the square root of 4*.

Mathematically it looks like this: $\sqrt{4} = 2$
(*root four equals two*).

9 is the square of 3, (3 x 3 = 9)
and so *3 is the square root of 9*.

The mathematical expression is $\sqrt{9} = 3$
(*root nine equals three*).

Squares

Complete the following: *e.g. $3^2 = 3 \times 3 = 9$*

a. $1^2 = $ ☐　　**b.** $2^2 = $ ☐　　**c.** $3^2 = $ ☐　　**d.** $4^2 = $ ☐

e. $5^2 = $ ☐　　**f.** $6^2 = $ ☐　　**g.** $7^2 = $ ☐　　**h.** $8^2 = $ ☐

i. $9^2 = $ ☐　　**j.** $10^2 = $ ☐　　**k.** $11^2 = $ ☐　　**l.** $12^2 = $ ☐

Cubes

Complete the following: *e.g. $4^3 = 4 \times 4 \times 4 = 64$* (Use grid at back to help you with difficult sums).

m. $1^3 = $ ☐　　**n.** $2^3 = $ ☐　　**o.** $3^3 = $ ☐　　**p.** $4^3 = $ ☐

q. $5^3 = $ ☐　　**r.** $6^3 = $ ☐　　**s.** $7^3 = $ ☐　　**t.** $8^3 = $ ☐

u. $9^3 = $ ☐　　**v.** $10^3 = $ ☐

Square roots

w. What is the square root of 16? ☐

x. What is $\sqrt{25}$? ☐　　　　**y.** What is $\sqrt{144}$? ☐

Complete the following: *e.g.* $\sqrt{16} + \sqrt{144}$, (4 x 4 = 16) therefore $\sqrt{16} = 4$
(12 x 12 = 144) therefore $\sqrt{144} = 12$,
4 + 12 = 16

z. $\sqrt{25} + \sqrt{144} = $ ☐　　**aa.** $\sqrt{144} - \sqrt{25} = $ ☐

bb. $\sqrt{64} \div \sqrt{4} = $ ☐　　**cc.** $\sqrt{81} \div \sqrt{9} = $ ☐

dd. $\sqrt{36} \times \sqrt{16} = $ ☐　　**ee.** $\sqrt{144} \div \sqrt{36} = $ ☐

ff. $\sqrt{1} + \sqrt{16} + \sqrt{49} = $ ☐

Mark your score out of 32:

＿＿＿
32

If you have got all the questions correct, colour in this star.

31

algebra

When you begin algebra you are embarking on a **quest into the unknown.** You have the treasure map, which shows **x** marking the spot. Now you have to sail to the desert island and find the spot marked by **x.** Only then will you know for certain how much the treasure is worth.
The **treasure may be worth only one**. If it is worth one, you can write **x = 1.**

In that case, **two treasures are worth two**, and you can write **2x = 2.**
In the same way it would be true to say that:

$$3x = 3,$$
$$4x = 4,$$
$$5x = 5, \text{ and so on.}$$

But if the **treasure is worth two**, you can write **x = 2.**
In this case, **2x = 4, 3x = 6, 4x = 8, 5x = 10**, and so on.

If the **treasure is worth three**, we can say **x = 3, 2x = 6, 3x = 9, 4x = 12, 5x = 15**, and so on.

The excitement of the treasure hunt is to find the treasure and see how much it is worth. **What is the value of x?**

If we are told that **4x = 20**, then we have been given an **equation**. To **solve the equation** is the same as finding **what x is worth**.

> **Important rule**

Look at the equation carefully: **4x = 20.**
It has a left-hand side (4x)   and a right-hand side (20).

There is a rule which says that you can **change the appearance of the equation, provided that you perform exactly the same operation to each side of the equation.**

If we **divide each side** of our equation (**4x = 20**) by **4**, the result is **x = 5.**

With a single step we have discovered the value of x.

Algebra

Treasure-hunting means finding out how much x is worth. Remember that it can be different in each treasure.

Find how much **x** is worth.

a. $2x = 4$
x = ☐

b. $2x = 6$
x = ☐

c. $2x = 8$
x = ☐

d. $3x = 6$
x = ☐

e. $3x = 9$
x = ☐

f. $3x = 12$
x = ☐

g. $3x = 15$
x = ☐

h. $3x = 18$
x = ☐

i. $3x = 21$
x = ☐

j. $3x = 24$
x = ☐

k. $3x = 27$
x = ☐

l. $3x = 30$
x = ☐

m. $4x = 8$
x = ☐

n. $4x = 12$
x = ☐

o. $4x = 16$
x = ☐

p. $5x = 10$
x = ☐

q. $5x = 15$
x = ☐

r. $5x = 20$
x = ☐

s. $6x = 18$
x = ☐

t. $6x = 24$
x = ☐

u. $6x = 30$
x = ☐

Mark
your score
out of 21:

———
21

If you have
got all the
questions
correct,
colour in
this star.

line graphs

Handling Data:

Data is information. Information reaches us in many ways: in words, numbers, in pictures, and in diagrams. Diagrams are a way of presenting information in a visual way that is easy to understand.

Line graphs, as well as pie charts and bar charts, present statistical information. Statistics is numerical information and it is often much easier to see the information on a chart or graph than as a list of figures.

This line graph shows the **increase in height of Johnny from the age of 2 to 18 years**.

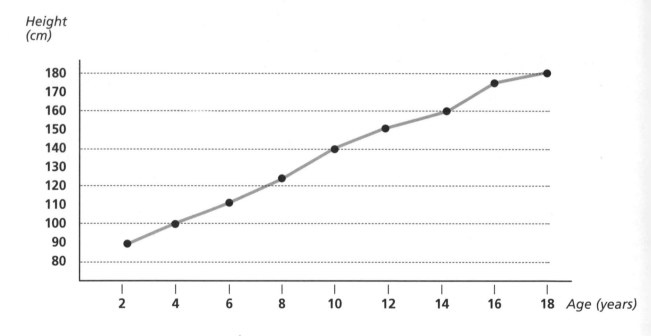

This graph shows a fairly **steady increase in height**.

We can see that **between the years of 2 and 18 Johnny grew from 90cm to 180cm**.
When Johnny was 10 his height was 140cm.
When Johnny was 14 his height was 160cm.

Line graphs

Line graphs are often used by businessess to show clearly and accurately how much profit they are making. Here is how one small ice cream company's profit was shown during the course of one year.
Remember ice cream does not sell so well when the weather is cold .

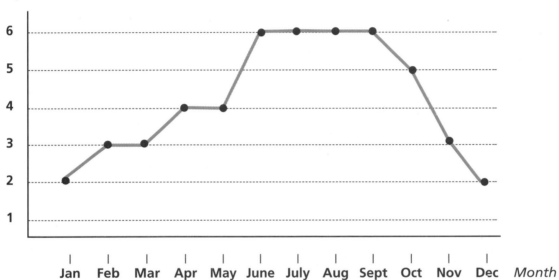

Profit (£1,000)

What was the profit in March?   _£3,000_

a. Which season of the year showed the highest profits ?   _ _ _ _ _ _ _

b. What was the profit in April?   _ _ _ _ _ _ _

c. How much higher was October's profit than May's?   _ _ _ _ _ _ _

d. Which 4 months showed the same profit?   _ _ _ _ _ _ _

e. Which months showed the lowest profit?   _ _ _ _ _ _ _

f. Why do you think profit was low in winter?   _ _ _ _ _ _ _

g. Why was the profit highest in June, July, August, September?   _ _ _ _ _ _ _

h. What was the profit in October?   _ _ _ _ _ _ _

i. Which months showed the same profit as November?   _ _ _ _ _ _ _

Mark your score out of 9:

_____
9

If you have got all the questions correct, colour in this star.

35

bar charts

A bar chart is another kind of diagram showing information in a way that is easy to understand.
A bar chart looks like a several blocks of flats in a line.
They do not quite touch each other, and some are taller than others. Again, it is very helpful to look at an example.

Example:
A Bar Chart of Favourite Colours
36 children were asked about their favourite colour. This bar chart gives us information about their answers.

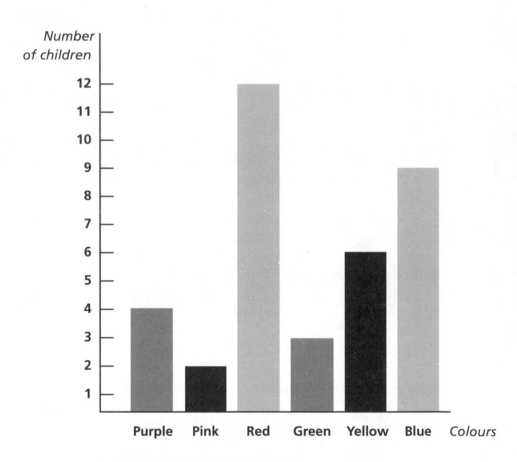

4 children like the colour purple
2 children like the colour pink
12 children like the colour red
3 children like the colour green
6 children like the colour yellow
9 children like the colour blue

It is easy to see that red was the most popular colour, and pink was the least popular.

Bar charts

a. 24 children were asked to name their favourite breed of dog.
Can you present their answers in a bar chart? Use the space below.

6 children like Collies
6 children like Dalmatians
4 children like Labradors
3 children like German Shepherds
3 children like Terriers
2 children like Saint Bernards

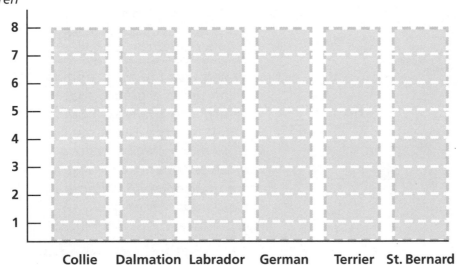

Number of children

Breed of dog

Collie · Dalmation · Labrador · German Shepherd · Terrier · St. Bernard

b. Which two dogs were the most popular? _ _ _ _ _ _ _

c. Which was the least popular? _ _ _ _ _ _ _

d. How many children liked Labradors? _ _ _ _ _ _ _

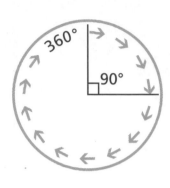

A pie chart is always in the form of a circle.
The different-sized slices of the pie present information in a way that is easy to understand.

It is important to remember that the movement all the way round the chart indicates **360°**.
So a slice of **36° is** $\frac{1}{10}$ **of the whole pie**, and a slice of **90° is** $\frac{1}{4}$ **of the whole pie**.

$$\frac{36}{360} = \frac{1}{10} \qquad \frac{90}{360} = \frac{1}{4}$$

This will become clear with the help of an example.

Example:
A Pie Chart of Favourite Colours
36 children were asked about their favourite colour.
This pie chart is a diagram of their answers.

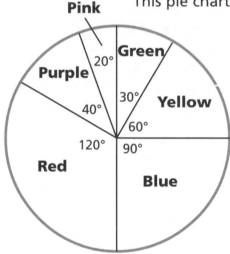

> understand the pie?

● *Which was the most popular colour?*
You can see at a glance that it was **red**.
● *Which was the least popular?*
Again, it is very easy to see that it was **pink**.
● *How many children chose blue?*
You can see that it was a **quarter**,
and a *quarter of 36 children* is **9 children**.
● *How many chose yellow?*
This is a little more difficult.

A slice of 60° is $\frac{1}{6}$ of the whole pie,
because $\frac{60°}{360} = \frac{1}{6}$

We just need to find $\frac{1}{6}$ *of the 36 children.*

Step 1 $\frac{60}{360} = \frac{1}{6}$	
Step 2 $\frac{1}{6}$ *of 36 = 6* $6\overline{)36}$ *= 6 children*	

Here is the full set of data presented by this pie chart:

Red (120°) = $\frac{1}{3}$ = 12 children   **Blue** (90°) = $\frac{1}{4}$ = 9 children

Yellow (60°) = $\frac{1}{6}$ = 6 children   **Purple** (40°) = $\frac{1}{9}$ = 4 children

Green (30°) = $\frac{1}{12}$ = 3 children   **Pink** (20°) = $\frac{1}{18}$ = 2 children

Total: 360° = 36 children

Pie charts

This pie chart shows what the weather was like for 12 days.

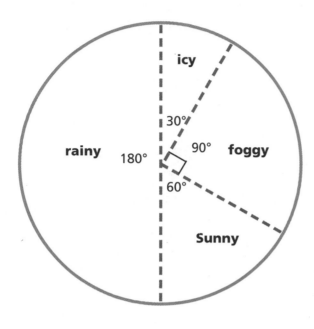

Tips:

$30° = \frac{1}{12}$

$60° = \frac{1}{6}$

$90° = \frac{1}{4}$

$180° = \frac{1}{2}$

a. On how many days did it rain? _ _ _ _ _ _ _ _ _ _

b. Were there more foggy days than sunny days? _ _ _ _ _ _ _ _ _ _

c. On how many days was it icy? _ _ _ _ _ _ _ _ _ _

d. How do you know by looking at the pie chart that there were more rainy days than sunny? _ _ _ _ _ _ _ _ _ _

e. Which two types of days added together come to the same amount as the foggy days? _ _ _ _ _ _ _ _ _ _

f. If there were twice as many sunny days as icy days how many more days was it sunny than icy? _ _ _ _ _ _ _ _ _ _

Mark your score out of 6:

___
6

If you have got all the questions correct, colour in this star.

39

probability

Probability tells you how likely it is that something will happen.

What are the chances of something happening?

For example: an ordinary pack of cards, without jokers, contains **52 cards**.
Half are red (*Hearts and Diamonds*) and
half are black (*Spades and Clubs*).

You shuffle the cards and take one at random.
● ***What are your chances of taking a black card?***
Because blacks and reds are equal (26 cards each)
the chance is equal.

Because there are *2 colours of equal quantity*,
the probability is 1 out of 2.

We can express this probability as $\frac{1}{2}$ or as **50%**.

● Now, ***what are your chances of drawing a Spade from a full pack?***

Because there are *4 suits* (*Spades, Clubs, Hearts and Diamonds*)
the chance is 1 out of 4,

which can be expressed as $\frac{1}{4}$ or **25%**.

● ***What are your chances of taking an ace?***
There is 1 ace in each suit.

Therefore there are a total of 4 (4 x 1) aces in a pack.
There are 4 chances out of 52.

$$= \frac{4}{52} = \frac{1}{13}$$

It is not all about cards, however. You can look at ***tossing a coin*** (*heads or tails*) or ***rolling a die to see which of the six numbers comes uppermost***.

And if you listen to weather reports, you will know that they often talk about the '***chances of rain***'. They have even created a new word to express the probability of rain.
They call it '***brollybility!***'

Cards

Imagine that you have shuffled the pack and are going to draw one card at random. Here are some questions about probability or chance. Give your answers as fractions.

a. What is the chance of drawing a *Diamond*?

b. What is the chance of drawing any *Seven*?

c. What is the chance of drawing either a *King* or a *Queen*?

d. What is the chance of drawing a *red card*?

e. What is the chance of drawing a *black card*?

Coins

f. When you toss a coin, what is the probability of *a head*?

Dice

g. What is the chance of throwing a *2*?

h. When you throw a dice, what is the chance of throwing an *even number*?

i. What is the chance of throwing an *odd number*?

j. What is the chance of throwing a *number above 3*?

k. What is the chance of throwing a 6?

Tip: When rolling dice you are just as likely to roll one number as any other. You are just as likely to roll a 6 as a 2. Because there are 6 numbers on the die, and each one is equally likely, then the probability of getting any number, say a '4' is 1 out of 6 or $\frac{1}{6}$.

Mark your score out of 11:

___
11

If you have got all the questions correct, colour in this star.

41

modes, means and medians

Modes, means and medians express different ways of looking at any group of numbers.

Let us look at a particular group of numbers:
11, **10**, **12**, **7**, **1**, **7**, **18**, **28**, **23**.

First we put them in order of size, beginning with the smallest:
1, **7**, **7**, **10**, **11**, **12**, **18**, **23**, **28**.

Now let us see how the **mode**, the **mean** and the **median** can be calculated for this group of numbers.

The mode

1, **7**, **7**, **10**, **11**, **12**, **18**, **23**, **28**.
Which number occurs most often in this group?
7 occurs twice, and each of the other numbers occurs only once.
So we have found *the mode*.
In this group of numbers the **mode is 7**.
The mode is therefore the number that appears most often.

The mean

1, **7**, **7**, **10**, **11**, **12**, **18**, **23**, **28**.
The mean is often called the average.
To find *the mean* of a group of numbers, *we add all the numbers together and divide the answer by the number of numbers*!
In our group of numbers the **total is 117**.
There are **9 numbers**, and so the **number of the numbers is 9**. *Divide the total (117) by 9, and the answer is 13.*
In this group of numbers the **mean** (*or average*) **is 13**.

The median

1, **7**, **7**, **10**, (**11**), **12**, **18**, **23**, **28**.

The median is the number which appears in the middle of the list.
11 appears in the middle. So we have found *the median*.
In this group of numbers the **median is 11**.

To obtain the median when there is no middle number (*for example*, if you have a group of 8 numbers), *find the two numbers closest to the middle, add them together and divide the answer by 2.*

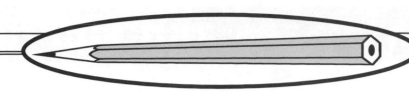

Modes, means and medians

Look at this group of numbers and then complete **a.** to **c.**

2, 5, 9, 12, 18, 18, 20.

a. In this group of numbers the mode is

b. In this group the mean is

c. In this group the median is

Look at this group of numbers and then complete **d.** to **f.**

4, 6, 6, 8, 12, 16, 18.

d. What is the mean?

e. What is the mode?

f. What is the median?

Look at this group of numbers and then complete **g.** to **i.**

1, 3, 5, 5, 8, 9, 11.

g. What is the median?

h. What is the mean?

i. What is the mode?

j. Tim saves some money every month. This is what he saved last year:

January	February	March	April	May	June
£2.50	£3	£1.50	£2	£5	£3

July	August	September	October	November	December
£1	£1	£3.50	£4	£3	£6.50

What is Tim's mean monthly saving?

Jack is 141cm tall. Fiona is 137cm. Claire is 133cm.

k. What is their mean height?

Mark your score out of 11:

_____

11

If you have got all the questions correct, colour in this star.

43

circles

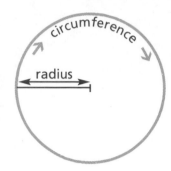

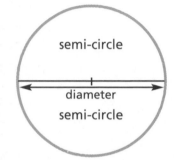

● *A circle is a wonderful shape*. It has no beginning and no end. Its centre is invisible. *The visible part is the line that goes all the way round this centre.* **This circular line is called the circumference**. All points on the circumference are equidistant (*at the same distance*) from the centre.

● **Any straight line from the centre to the circumference is called the radius** (r). The plural of radius is radii (*Ray-Dee-Eye*).

● **Any straight line going right across the circle and passing through the centre is called the diameter**.

● The diameter (d) is twice as long as the radius (d = 2r). The diameter cuts the circle into two halves. **Each half is called a semi-circle**.

Calculating the circumference

If we know the **radius** (r) of a circle, we can calculate the length of the circumference. *We use a special formula*. The formula has a strange ingredient. This ingredient is a Greek letter called Pi (Pie). In Greek Pi looks like this: π.
Pi stands for a number which is approximately 3.14.
The *'special formula'* for calculating the circumference (c) of a circle is **$2\pi r$**. This means 2 x 3.14 x **radius**.

$$c = 2\pi r$$

● *For example:* The radius of a circle is 5cm.
What is the circumference?
Answer: **The circumference = $2\pi r$ = 2 x 3.14 x 5cm**
= 3.14 x 10cm
= 31.4cm.

Calculating the Area of a Circle

$$\text{area} = \pi r^2$$

The *'special formula'* for calculating the area (a) of a circle is πr^2.
πr^2 is a formula that tells us to multiply π by the radius, and *then multiply the answer by the radius again*.
This means πr^2 = 3.14 x **radius** x **radius**.
So, if we have the radius we can find the area.

● *For example:* The radius of a circle is 2cm.
What is the area of the circle?
Answer: **The area = πr^2 = 3.14 x 2cm x 2cm**
= 3.14 x 4cm^2
= 12.56 cm^2
(*Remember: The area has to be expressed in cm²*)

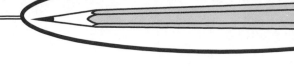

Radii and diameters

Remembering that the diameter of a circle is twice as long as the radius (d = 2r), complete this table:

	radius	diameter			radius	diameter
a.	2cm		**g.**			1cm
b.		3cm	**h.**		2.25cm	
c.	6cm		**i.**			6cm
d.		10cm	**j.**		1.4cm	
e.	3.5cm		**k.**			4cm
f.		2.5cm	**l.**		5.1cm	

Circumference

Using the formula $2\pi r$, fill in the blanks, use a calculator to help you:

	radius	circumference			radius	circumference
m.	1cm		**q.**		0.5cm	
n.	2cm		**r.**		1.5cm	
o.	3cm		**s.**		2.5cm	
p.	4cm		**t.**		3.5cm	

Area of Circles

Using the formula πr^2, fill in the blanks, use a calculator to help you:

	radius	area			radius	area
u.	1cm		**x.**		4cm	
v.	2cm		**y.**		5cm	
w.	3cm		**z.**		6cm	

Mark your score out of 26:

_____
26

If you have got all the questions correct, colour in this star.

45

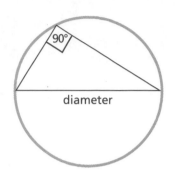

Semi-circles

We already know that *half a circle is called a* **semi-circle** and that it is *produced by drawing a diameter*.
But here is something amazing:
any triangle with the diameter as its base and *with its third point anywhere on the circumference will always be a right-angled triangle*.
That is, the angle at the point on the circumference will always be 90°.

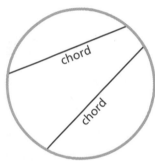

Chords

A **chord** *is a straight line joining any two points on the circumference of a circle*.

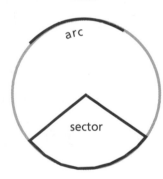

Arcs

An **arc** *is any part of the circumference*.

Sectors

A **sector** is like a slice of pizza. *It has two straight sides, which are radii. It also has a curved side, which is an arc.*

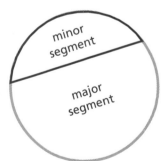

Segments

A **segment** is a different kind of slice. *It has two edges. The straight edge is a chord, and the curved edge is an arc.*

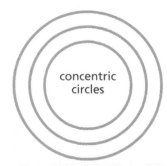

Concentric circles

Concentric circles *are two or more circles with the same centre.*

a. With ruler and pencil
1. draw a diameter for this circle. Use this **diameter** as the base of a triangle.
2. Choose any point on the circumference and draw two straight lines from this point to the two ends of the diameter.
3. With your protractor check that the angle at the circumference is 90°.

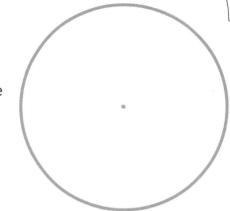

b. With ruler and pencil draw a **chord** in this circle.

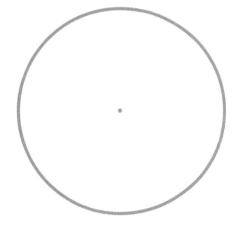

c. With ruler and pencil draw a **sector** in this circle.

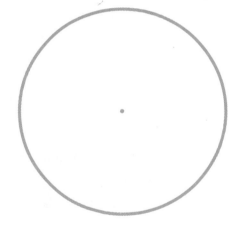

d. With ruler and pencil draw a **segment** in this circle.

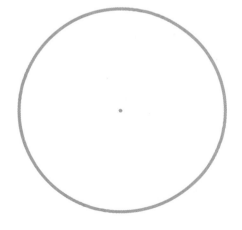

e. With a pair of compasses draw two circles with the same centre as this circle.

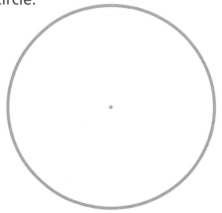

Mark your score out of 5:

_____
5

If you have got all the questions correct, colour in this star.

triangles

*A **triangle, as its name tells us, has three angles**.*
These angles are produced by its three sides.
The astonishing fact about **these angles is that they always total 180°**, no matter what shape the triangle may be!

Right-angled Triangles

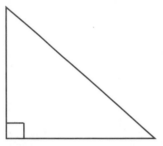

We have already seen that right-angled triangles can be drawn within a semi-circle.
Two essential facts about a right-angled triangle are :
1. **One of its angles must be 90°** (*a right angle*).
2. ***The sum of its other two angles is always 90°** (90° + 90° =180°).*

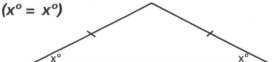

Equilateral Triangles

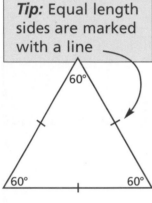

Tip: Equal length sides are marked with a line

This name also explains itself. **An equilateral triangle has three equal sides.** This means that its three angles are also equal. **Every angle is therefore 60°**, no matter the size of the triangle.

Isosceles Triangles

*An **isosceles** (Eye-Soss-A-Lees) **triangle has two sides of equal length. The third side can be longer or shorter.** The two angles opposite the two equal sides are also equal. (x° = x°)*

Scalene Triangles

*A **scalene** (Skay-Lean) **triangle has no equal sides and therefore no equal angles.***

When you feel you are ready for this practice, cover the left-hand page and write the correct name (with correct spelling!) for each of these triangles.

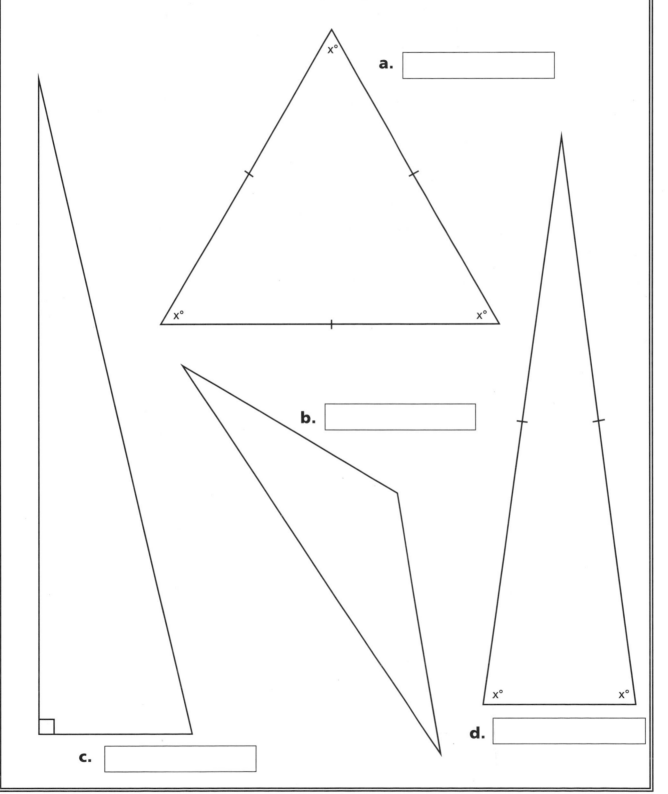

a. [   ]

b. [   ]

c. [   ]

d. [   ]

Mark your score out of 4:

___
4

If you have got all the questions correct, colour in this star.

49

triangle measurements

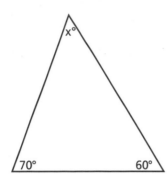

Angles

You remember that *the three angles of any triangle total 180°*.

In this **scalene** triangle, therefore, we can work out the mystery angle by adding the two known angles and taking the answer away from 180°, like this:

70° + 60° = 130°
180° – 130° = 50°
Answer: **x = 50°**

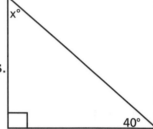

● It is even easier with **right-angled triangles**. Simply take the other known angle (in this case, 40°) away from 90° (90° – 40°).
Answer: **x = 50°**

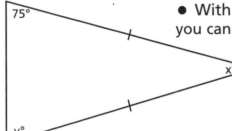

● With **isosceles** *triangles,* if there is one known angle, you can work out the other two angles.

● *Example 1:*
Angle **y** is one of the equal angles, and so it must be **75°**. The two equal angles therefore total **150°**. Therefore angle **x = 180° – 150° = 30°**

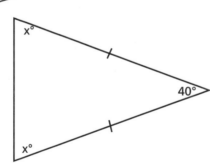

● *Example 2:*
By taking 40° from 180° we find that the total of **x and y is 140°**. But **x** and **y** are equal, and so each is $\frac{140°}{2}$ = **70°**.

Equilateral triangles are the easiest of all, because each angle is always 60°.

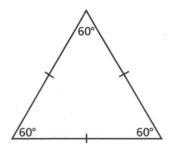

Angles

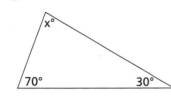

a. In this **scalene** triangle x = ☐

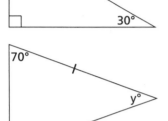

b. In this **right-angled** triangle x = ☐

c. In this **isosceles** triangle x = ☐

and y = ☐

d. In this **isosceles** triangle x = ☐

and y = ☐

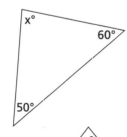

e. In this **scalene** triangle x = ☐

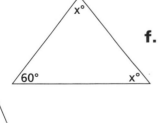

f. In this **equilateral** triangle x = ☐

g. In this **right-angled** triangle x = ☐

Mark your score out of 7:

——
7

If you have got all the questions correct, colour in this star.

51

Areas

To find the **area** of a triangle, *multiply the base* (b) *by the height* (h), *and divide the answer by 2*: $\frac{(b \times h)}{2}$.

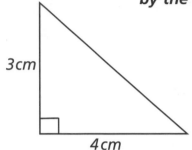

3cm

4cm

Right-angled Triangles

This is easy with a right-angled triangle because one of its sides is the base and the side at right angles to the base is the height. Formula: $\frac{(b \times h)}{2}$

In this example the **area** = $\frac{4 \times 3}{2}$ = 6 cm^2.

Other Triangles

With all other triangles you need:
1. *to be able to work out the height first*
or 2. *to be told the height*.

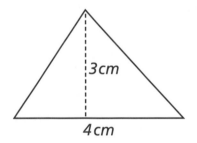

3cm

4cm

● *Example 1*
Here we are told that the base is 4cm, and the dotted line gives the height as 3cm.
So the area = $\frac{4 \times 3}{2}$ = 6cm^2.

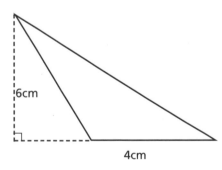

6cm

4cm

● *Example 2*
We are told that the base is 4cm.
The dotted line shows a height of 6cm.
So the area = $\frac{4 \times 6}{2}$ = 12cm^2.

Areas

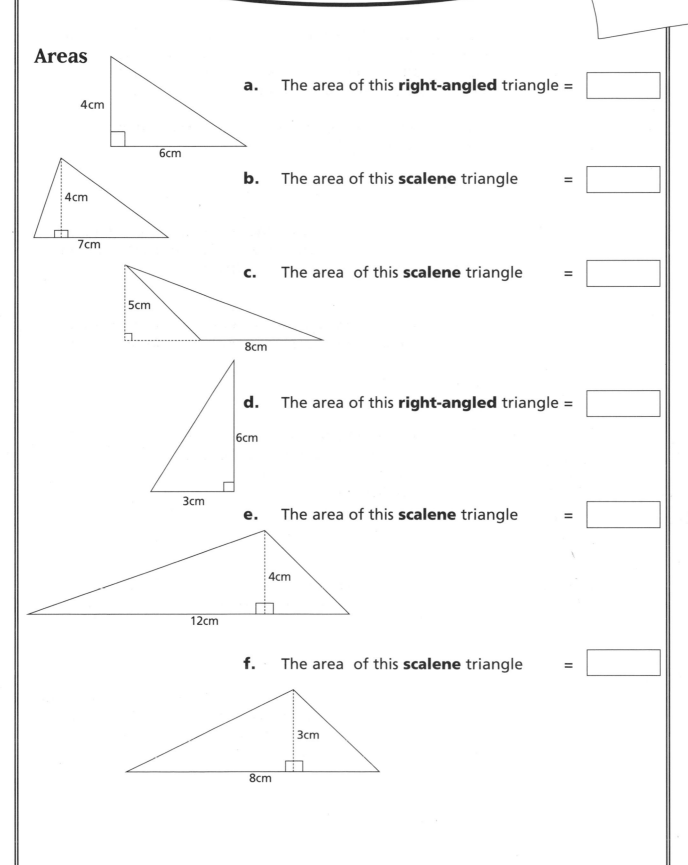

a. The area of this **right-angled** triangle =

b. The area of this **scalene** triangle =

c. The area of this **scalene** triangle =

d. The area of this **right-angled** triangle =

e. The area of this **scalene** triangle =

f. The area of this **scalene** triangle =

Mark your score out of 6:

—
6

If you have got all the questions correct, colour in this star.

quadrilaterals

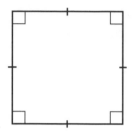

Every quadrilateral has four straight sides. It also has four angles. When we add the four angles together we always get a **total of 360°**. There are different kinds of quadrilaterals. One of the most familiar is the square.

- **A square** *has four right angles, and its four sides are all the same length*.

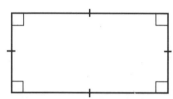

- Another well-known quadrilateral is the **rectangle**.
A **rectangle** *also has four right angles, but one pair of parallel sides is longer than the other pair.*

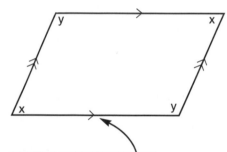

- **A parallelogram** *has two pairs of parallel sides, but no right angles. Its opposite angles are equal.*

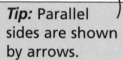

Tip: Parallel sides are shown by arrows.

- **A rhombus** *is a parallelogram which has all its sides of the same length.* It helps to think of it as a diamond.

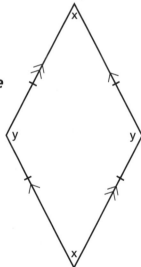

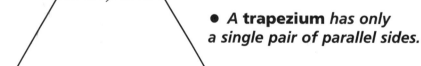

- **A trapezium** *has only a single pair of parallel sides.*

- **A kite** *has two sides of equal length that touch each other and two longer sides of equal length that also touch each other.*

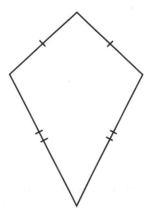

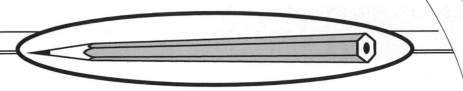

When you are ready for this practice, cover the left-hand page and write the correct name (*with correct spelling!*)

a.

b.

c.
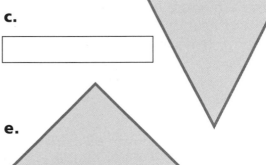

d.
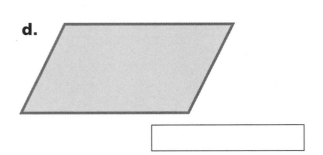

e.
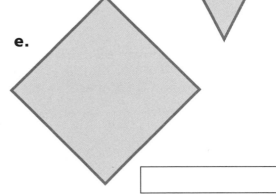

f.
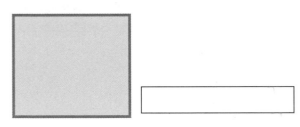

Which quadrilaterals are being described?
Write their names, correctly spelt, in the boxes.

g. This has two pairs of parallel sides but no right angles.

h. This has only one pair of parallel sides.

i. This has four right angles and all its sides equal.

j. This has two pairs of sides of equal length but no parallel lines.

k. This has a diamond shape.

l. This has four right angles and two pairs of parallel lines.

polygons

A **polygon** *is any two-dimensional shape made of three or more straight sides.*

This means that a triangle is a polygon, and a square is also a polygon. *But we normally think of polygons as shapes with five or more sides*. We are going to concentrate on regular polygons. In *a regular* **polygon** *all the sides are the same length and all the angles are equal*.

We already know that in an equilateral triangle each angle is 60° and that in a square each angle is 90°. So let us look at some other regular polygons and their angles.

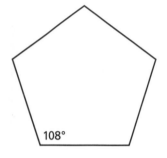

● *A pentagon has five sides. Each angle is 108°.* The Pentagon is the name given to the central offices of the US military and defence department, consisting of five pentagonal buildings.

● *A hexagon has six sides. Each angle is 120°.* Many pencils have a hexagonal section to prevent them from rolling too readily. Bees construct their wax combs with hexagonal compartments for the storage of nectar.

● *A heptagon has seven sides. Each angle is 128.57°!* A 50p coin is in the shape of a heptagon, although the seven sides are all slightly curved.

● *An octagon has eight sides*, just as an octopus has eight tentacles. *Each angle is 135°.* October used to be the eighth month, and people in their eighties are octogenarians.

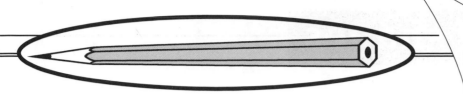

When you are ready for this practice, cover the left-hand page.
Next to each shape write its correct name.

a.

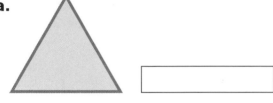

b.

c.

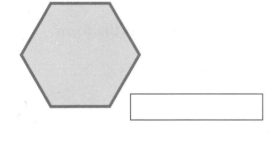

d.

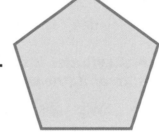

e.

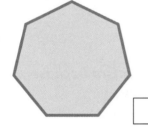

f.

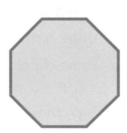

g. What is the shape of a 50p coin?

h. Which polygon is used by bees?

i. Which polygon gives its name to a group of buildings
in the USA?

j. Which shape is often used in the manufacture of pencils?

k. Which shape has some connection with a sea-creature?

Mark
your score
out of II:

———
II

If you have
got all the
questions
correct,
colour in
this star.

3-D shapes

3-D means three-dimensional. Thus 3-D shapes have three dimensions: length, width and height. A brick has a 3-D shape. So does a piece of seaside rock. You can see why 3-D shapes are sometimes called **solids**. Some familiar 3-D shapes:

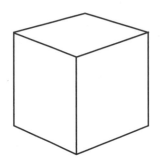

- *A **cube** has six faces.* Each face is a square.

    sugar cubes

    a baby's building bricks

- *A **cuboid** also has six faces, but the faces are all rectangles.*

    builders' bricks

    video cassettes

- *A **cylinder** is sometimes called a circular prism because any slice of it (the cross section) is always a circle.*

    Swiss rolls

    spaghetti

- *A **triangular prism** has a cross section in the form of a triangle.*

    ridge tents

    some chocolate bar containers

- *This **pyramid** has a square base and four identical triangular faces.* The world-famous example is the Great Pyramid in Egypt.

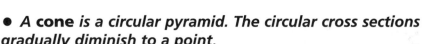
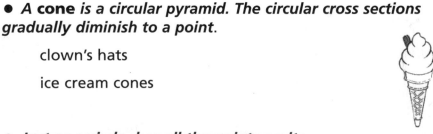

- *A **cone** is a circular pyramid. The circular cross sections gradually diminish to a point.*

    clown's hats

    ice cream cones

- *Just as a circle, has all the points on its circumference equidistant from the centre, so a **sphere** has all the points on the surface equidistant from the centre.*

When you are ready for this practice, cover the left-hand page.
Now see how many of these questions you can answer.
Some answers are on the previous page; some you have to work out.

a. What does 3-D mean? _

b. How many faces does a cube have? _ _ _ _ _ _ _

c. What shape is each face on a cube? _ _ _ _ _ _ _

d. What shape is each face on a cuboid? _ _ _ _ _ _ _

e. How many edges does a cuboid have? _ _ _ _ _ _ _

f. What is a more common name for a circular prism? _ _ _ _ _ _ _

g. Which shape has rectangular faces? _ _ _ _ _ _ _

h. How many faces does a triangular prism have? _ _ _ _ _ _ _

i. How many faces does a square-based pyramid have? _ _ _ _ _ _ _

Can you complete these shapes with your pencil?

j. cylinder

k. cuboid

l. Cone

m. triangular prism

n. cube

o. square-based pyramid

symmetry

The word symmetry means: an exact correspondance in position or form about a given point, line or plane.

The diameter of a circle produces two precise semi-circles. **It is as if one semi-circle is reflected in a mirror.** The second semi-circle is a reflection of the first. **This is an example of reflective symmetry.** The mirror (in this case the diameter) is called the **line of symmetry**.

 **Reflective symmetry**

A rectangle has 2 lines of symmetry.

1. You might be asked to draw a mirror image of this shape:

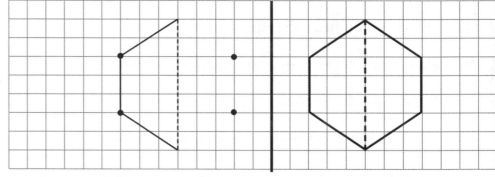

2. The top of the vertical line is 3 squares to the left of the line of symmetry.

3. Mark a point 3 squares to the right on the same horizontal. Mark a similar point to match the bottom of the vertical line. Join the points.

 **Rotational symmetry**

Rotational *means turning. Let us find out how it works.*

Take a square piece of card. Pin it through its centre to a larger piece of card. With your pencil draw round the outside of the square, leaving its outline on the larger card. As you turn the square card round on its central pin, you will find that there are three more positions where it completely fills the pencil square you have drawn on the larger card. Because there are four positions altogether where the square occupies the same outline, we say that *a square has an order of rotation of 4.*

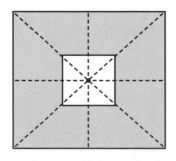

Tip: The lines of reflective symmetry will tell you the order of rotation.

Most shapes, if turned, merely look different. Such shapes have an **order of rotation of 1**. In other words, *they do not have rotational symmetry.*

Reflective Symmetry

a. How many lines of symmetry does a square have?

b. Draw the lines of symmetry in this square.

c. How many lines of symmetry does a regular hexagon have?

d. Draw the lines of symmetry in this hexagon.

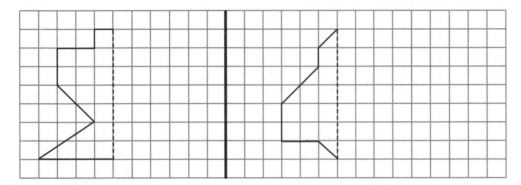

e. Draw the mirror image

f. Draw the mirror image

Rotational Symmetry

Try these with pieces of card. When turning your card-shape, make sure you know when you get back to the starting position, but do not count the starting position twice!

Tip: The centre is where the diagonals cross.

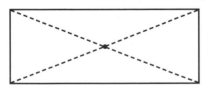

g. What is the order of rotation of a rectangle?

h. What is the order of rotation of an equilateral triangle?

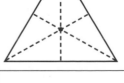

Tip: Mark the midpoint of each side. Join these points to the angles opposite. Where the dotted lines cross is the centre. You can also see how each dotted line is a line of symmetry.

i. What is the order of rotation of a regular hexagon? The centre is where any two lines of symmetry cross.

Mark your score out of 9:

_____
9

If you have got all the questions correct, colour in this star.

61

patterns

A pattern is a particular shape or design which appeals to us. Millions of patterns are produced by nature: A spider's web, frost on the windows, the flight formation of geese, the double-helix structure of the DNA molecule, the wind patterns around the earth, the tidal movements in the oceans, the shapes of clouds, and the swirling arms of spiral galaxies.

Patterns are also designed by people. These range from repetitive patterns on wall paper to the patterns of a school day, a school term, and a school year.

Repeating patterns

Many patterns have a simple design which keeps repeating.

Symmetrical patterns

Other patterns are symmetrical. Some have **one line of symmetry**, some have **two lines of symmetry**.

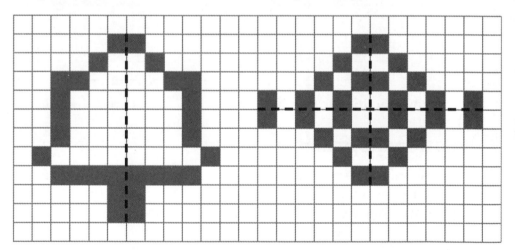

Tessellation

Tessellation *is a pattern made of shapes that fit snugly together.* When the pattern is made of a single repeating shape, it is called *tiling.* A good example of tiling is the wax honeycomb made by bees and based on the hexagon.

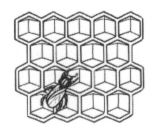

But tessellation may consist of more than one shape. Black squares and white octagons go well together to produce a pleasing pattern for floor tiling.

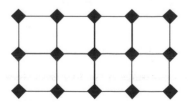

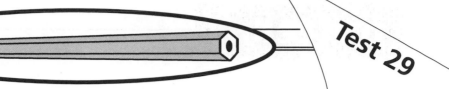

Repeating Patterns

Design two simple repeating patterns.

Symmetrical Patterns

a. Complete this pattern, which has one line of symmetry.

b. Complete this pattern, which has two lines of symmetry.

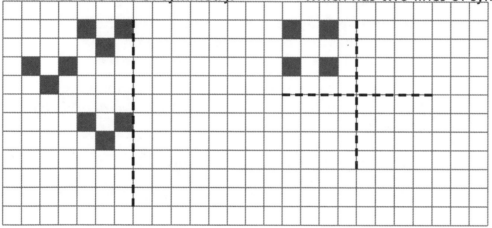

Tessellation

Continue these two patterns.

c.

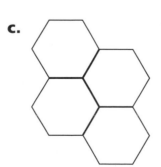

length

Everything in the universe is measured. Human beings love checking the measurements for themselves.

A castaway marooned on a desert island cuts notches in a stick to record the passing days. Millions of bathroom scales are used every day. People glance at their watches to check the time.

Let us consider first how we **measure length and distance.**

Units of length

Look at the smallest division of space on your ruler. This space measures **one millimetre**. If you look carefully, you will see that **ten of these divisions make 1cm.**

Your teacher may have a **1-metre ruler** in the classroom. This ruler has **100 centimetres** marked on it, because **100 centimetres make 1 metre.**

If your school is **1 kilometre** from your home, this is the distance measured by laying **1000 such rulers end to end in a long line**!

Here is the length chart to help you:

	Abbreviation	Full form	Meaning
1000mm = 1m 10mm = 1cm	mm	millimetre	one thousandth of a metre
100cm = 1m	cm	centimetre	one hundredth of a metre
1000m = 1km	km	kilometre	one thousand metres

'**Conversion**' means '**changing.**'
Here are the rules for changing units of length.
To change:

kilometres to **metres**, multiply by 1,000 (*2km = 2,000m*)

metres to **centimetres**, multiply by 100 (*3.5m = 350cm*)

centimetres to **millimetres**, multiply by 10 (*1.5cm = 15mm*)

millimetres to **centimetres**, divide by 10 (*25mm = 2.5cm*)

centimetres to **metres**, divide by 100 (*145cm = 1.45m*)

metres to **kilometres**, divide by 1,000 (*2,325m = 2.325km*)

Units of Length

Which unit of length is the most suitable for measuring

a. a train journey?

b. the length of a swimming pool?

c. the length of a lorry?

d. the height of a tree?

e. the length of a pencil?

f. the thickness of cardboard?

g. the diameter of your pencil lead?

Conversion

See if you can follow the conversion rules by filling in the blanks correctly.

h. 3km = _____ m

i. 2m = _____ cm

j. 2.5cm = _____ mm

k. 4.5km = _____ m

l. 6.25m = _____ cm

m. 2.6cm = _____ mm

n. 35mm = _____ cm

o. 150cm = _____ m

p. 1250m = _____ km

q. 350mm = _____ cm

r. 748cm = _____ m

s. 10672m = _____ km

t. 3000mm = _____ cm

u. 1km = _____ m

v. 42cm = _____ mm

w. 3600m = _____ km

x. 862cm = _____ mm

y. 2.1km = _____ m

z. 500mm = _____ cm

Mark your score out of 26:

_____
26

If you have got all the questions correct, colour in this star.

mass

Measures of mass

Even though *an elephant is massive, we talk about its weight rather than its mass*; but we talk about the *mass of the planet Saturn*.

Weight is a more general, although technically incorrect word, and **mass** is a more precise, scientific term.

Here is the chart to help you with mass.
The basic unit is the **gram**.

	Abbreviation	Full form	Meaning
1,000mg = 1g	mg	milligram	one thousandth of a gram
1000g = 1kg	kg	kilogram	one thousand grams
1,000kg = 1t	t	tonne	

Conversion rules

To change:
tonnes to **kilograms**, multiply by 1,000 (*2t = 2,000kg*)
kilograms to **grams**, multiply by 1,000 (*3kg = 3,000g*)
grams to **milligrams**, multiply by 1,000 (*0.75g = 750mg*)
milligrams to **grams**, divide by 1,000 (*350mg = 0.35g*)
grams to **kilograms**, divide by 1,000 (*500g = 0.5kg*)
kilograms to **tonnes**, divide by 1,000 (*400kg = 0.4t*)

Measures of capacity

Measures of capacity are normally used for liquids such as petrol and milk. In these cases the basic unit is the litre, but millilitres can be used for medicines.

	Abbreviation	Full form	Meaning
1000ml = 1l 10ml = 1cl	ml	millilitre	one thousandth of a litre
100cl = 1l	cl	centilitre	one hundredth of a litre
1,000ml = 1l	l	litre	

Conversion rules

See if you can work out the six rules for capacity conversion. Here are the first 2:

To change:
litres to **centilitres**, multiply by 100 (*2l = 200cl*)
centilitres to **millilitres**, multiply by 10 (*30cl = 300ml*)

Measures of Mass

Which measure of mass is the most suitable for weighing

a. a bag of potatoes?

b. a ship?

c. a chocolate bar?

d. a vitamin C tablet?

Fill in the blanks:

e. 1.5kg = _____ g

f. 250mg = _____ g

g. 1300kg = _____ t

h. 1.5t = _____ kg

i. 0.35g = _____ mg

j. 1200g = _____ kg

k. 3.5kg = _____ g

l. 2t = _____ kg

m. 0.05g = _____ mg

n. 300g = _____ kg

Measure of Capacity

Which measure of capacity would you use when:

o. Putting petrol in the car?

p. Buying milk in the supermarket?

q. Administering medicines?

Fill in the blank, using the capacity conversion rules that you have worked out:

r. 2l = _____ ml

s. 2l = _____ cl

t. 500ml = _____ l

u. 7cl = _____ ml

v. 800ml = _____ cl

w. 450cl = _____ l

x. 50l = _____ cl

y. 300ml = _____ cl

Mark your score out of 25:

_____
25

If you have got all the questions correct, colour in this star.

67

time

Time is a mysterious concept. *Every movement in the universe takes a certain time to be completed.*
In fact, *movement* and *moment* are really the same word.
Yet we think of seconds rather than moments when we want to measure time.
Some scientists deal with nanoseconds, which are units of time so short that you need one thousand million of them to make just one second!

We are going to start our chart with the second as the basic unit.

60 seconds	=	1 minute	365 days = 1 year
60 minutes	=	1 hour	366 days = 1 leap year
24 hours	=	1 day	10 years = 1 decade
7 days	=	1 week	100 years = 1 century
14 days	=	1 fortnight	1000 years = 1 millennium

Calendar

There is an old rhyme to help us remember how many days there are in each calendar month:

> *Thirty days* hath *September, April, June* and *November,*
> All the rest have *thirty-one,* Excepting *February* alone,
> Which has *twenty-eight days* clear,
> And *twenty-nine* in *each leap year.*

Clocks and watches

Analogue clocks and watches have hands that move round a face.
They work on a **12-hour system**, where
a.m. means *before midday* and *p.m.* means *after midday.*

Digital clocks and watches use a 24-hour system.
They do not need *a.m.* or *p.m.* because any number
after 12 indicates a time between midday and midnight.
So **15.00** means **3p.m.** (*15 - 12 = 3*).

Working out time

*Example: **A film starts at 8.15 and finishes at 10.30.***
How long did the film last?

```
  10h  30mins.
-  8h  15mins.
= 2h  15mins.
```

However, if the film started at 8.40, you would need to borrow an hour from the hour's column.

```
  10h  30mins.        Because you cannot subtract 40 from 30
-  8h  40mins.        you need to borrow an hour = 60mins.
                      This means that you subtract 1 from
   9h  90mins.        the hour column and add 60 to the
-  8h  40mins.        minutes column.
=  1h  50mins.
```

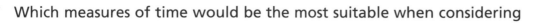

Which measures of time would be the most suitable when considering

a. your school's summer holiday?

b. a 100-metre race?

c. your time in Junior School?

d. a family holiday abroad?

e. periods of time like the 1990s?

f. longer historical periods?

g. a period of 1000 years?

h. A lesson begins at 9.35 and ends at 10.10. How long is the lesson?

i. A Schools TV programme starts at 9.20 and ends at 10.40. How long is the programme?

j. When Mr Dawson was ill he had five days off work. His first day off was September 28. On what date did he return to work?

k. Mum puts the cake into the oven at 2.20p.m. It stays there for $2\frac{3}{4}$ hrs. At what time does Mum take the cake out of the oven?

Fill in the blanks. *Remember to use **a.m.** or **p.m.** when necessary.*

	12-hour system	24-hour clock
l.	7.50a.m.	_ _ _ _ _ _
m.	_ _ _ _ _ _	16:48
n.	8.27p.m.	_ _ _ _ _ _
o.	_ _ _ _ _ _	13:01
p.	6.05p.m.	_ _ _ _ _ _
q.	_ _ _ _ _ _	23:59

Mark your score out of 17:

_____

17

If you have got all the questions correct, colour in this star.

69

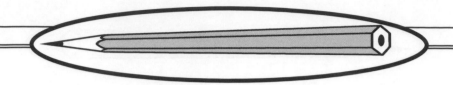

Revision Practice

To gain the most benefit from this practice it is a good idea to go through these steps, in order.

Method

> **Step 1** — Look carefully at all we have done so far. Check that you understand **the facts** and know how to do **the practice**.

> **Step 2** — Try answering all the questions as if you were taking a test at school. See how many you can do confidently.

> **Step 3** — Do any working on paper. If you have any uncertainties, use the earlier part of the book to help you complete your answers.

> **Step 4** — Check your answers with those at the back of the book.

Practice

a. What is the value of 7 in the number 3672?

b. 44 rounded to the nearest 10 is

c. 36 rounded to the nearest 10 is

d. 454 rounded to the nearest 100 is

e. 317 + 249 + 12 + 1706 =

f. 2025 – 1462 =

g. 34 x 17 =

h. 692 x 38 =

i. 72 oranges in each box. How many in 25 boxes?

j. 2487 ÷ 15 =

k. 5209 ÷ 17 =

l. £4000 is shared equally among 20 charities. How much does each charity receive?

m. Concert tickets are £14 each. The management have takings of £2800. How many tickets have been sold?

n. Continue the sequence
13 26 39 ☐ ☐ ☐

o. The factors of 18 are
☐ ☐ ☐ ☐ ☐ ☐

p. The factors of 35 are
☐ ☐ ☐ ☐

q. 22, 33, 44 are all multiples of

r. 1 is the first prime number. True or false?

s. The prime factors of 24 are

t. 8 is not a prime factor of 32. True or false?

u. 0.5 is bigger than 0.06. True or false?

v. Put in order, beginning with the smallest: $\frac{1}{2}$ $\frac{1}{4}$ $\frac{1}{3}$

w. A fraction is a

x. The most common fraction is a

y. The decimal form for a tenth is

z. The decimal form for a hundredth is

aa. The percentage form for a hundredth is

bb. The top part of a fraction is called the

cc. The bottom part of a fraction is called

dd. Express $\frac{1}{2}$ in decimal form

ee. Express $\frac{1}{2}$ in percentage form

ff. Express 0.75 as a percentage

gg. $\frac{2}{9} + \frac{2}{9} =$

hh. $\frac{4}{7} + \frac{1}{7} =$

ii. $\frac{1}{2} + \frac{1}{3} =$

jj. $\frac{1}{2} - \frac{1}{3} =$

kk. $\frac{1}{4} \times \frac{1}{5} =$

ll. $\frac{2}{5} \times \frac{1}{2} = *$

mm. $\frac{8}{9} \times \frac{3}{4} = *$

nn. $\frac{1}{9} \div \frac{1}{4} =$

oo. $\frac{5}{18} \div \frac{2}{9} =$

pp. 0.27 + 0.47 =

qq. 0.674 + 0.528 =

rr. 0.835 − 0.679 =

ss. 0.625 x 10 =

tt. 0.625 x 100 =

uu. 0.625 ÷ 10 =

vv. 0.625 ÷ 100 =

ww. What is 3% of £100?

xx. Half of £1

yy. Half of £3

zz. Double 75

ab. Double 5mm

ac. Half of 3.2

ad. 2^2

ae. 5^2

af. $\sqrt{36}$

ag. 3^3

ah. 2x = 10   x =

71

Handling data

36 children were asked to name their favourite fruit. This pie chart is a diagram of their answers.

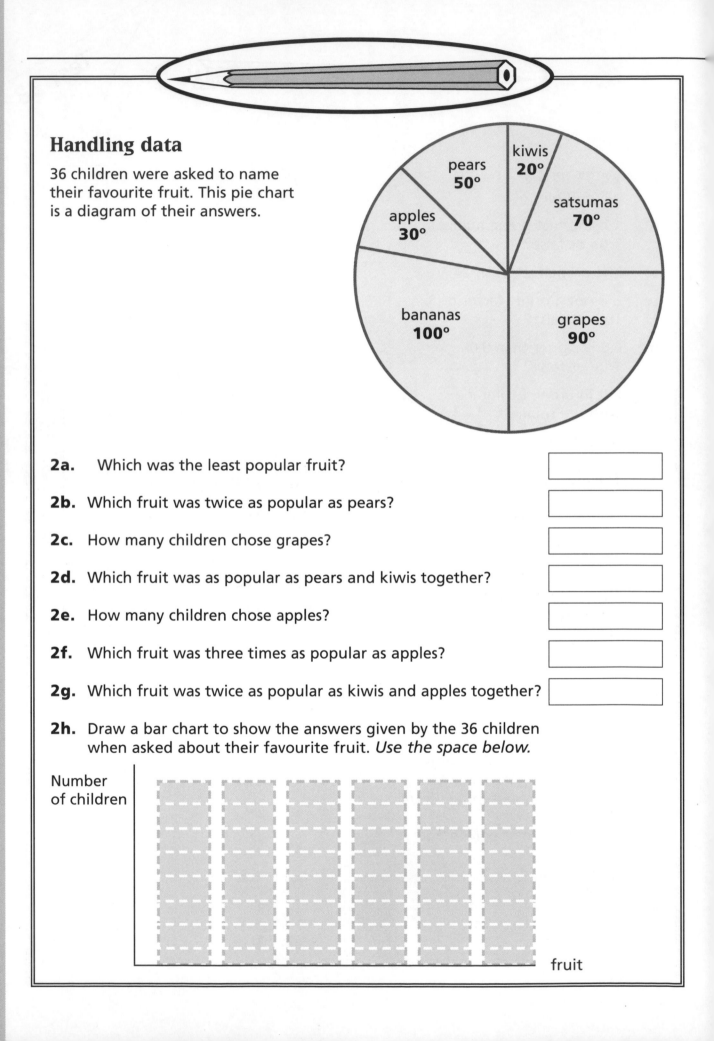

pears 50°

kiwis 20°

apples 30°

satsumas 70°

bananas 100°

grapes 90°

2a. Which was the least popular fruit?

2b. Which fruit was twice as popular as pears?

2c. How many children chose grapes?

2d. Which fruit was as popular as pears and kiwis together?

2e. How many children chose apples?

2f. Which fruit was three times as popular as apples?

2g. Which fruit was twice as popular as kiwis and apples together?

2h. Draw a bar chart to show the answers given by the 36 children when asked about their favourite fruit. *Use the space below.*

Number of children

fruit

Models, Means and Medians

Look at this group of numbers and then complete **2i – 2l**

3   4   6   9   7   8   5   6   6

2i. In this group of numbers the mode is

2j. The mean is

2k. The median is

2l. Jenny's marks in 5 history tests were
54% 63% 58% 71% 64%.
What was Jenny's average history test mark?

Geometry: Circles

3a. Name the circular line forming the outer limit of a circle.

3b. A straight line from the centre of a circle to the outside
is called the

3c. A straight line going right across a circle and passing
through the centre is called the

3d. The proper name for half a circle is

3e. What is the formula for calculating the circumference
of a circle?

3f. What is the formula for calculating the area of a circle?

3g. Which alphabet does π belong to?

3h. If the radius is 1.2cm, the diameter is

3i. If the diameter is 4.9cm. the radius is

3j. The diameter of a circle forms the base of a triangle.
What is the measurement of the angle which touches
the circumference?

3k. What is the name of a straight line joining any two points
on the circumference of a circle?

3l. How many straight sides does a sector have?

3m. Circles with the same centre are called

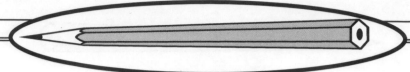

Triangles

4a. How many angles does a triangle have?

4b. The angles of any triangle total

4c. What is the name of a triangle that has one angle of 90°?

4d. A triangle with all its sides equal is called an ⬚ triangle.

4e. What does each angle measure when the sides of a triangle are all equal?

4f. A triangle with two sides equal is known as an ⬚ triangle.

4g. A triangle with no equal sides is called a ⬚ triangle.

4h. A triangle with two sides equal also has two ⬚ equal.

4i. A triangle has an angle of 71° and another of 46°. What is the third angle?

4j. What is the area of a triangle with a base of 6cm and a height of 4cm?

Quadrilaterals & Polygons

4k. How many sides does a quadrilateral have?

4l. How many pairs of parallel lines does a square have?

4m. A quadrilateral with only one pair of parallel lines is called a

4n. A parallelogram that looks like a diamond is a

4o. This has four right angles and two pairs of parallel lines.

4p. This has four right angles and all its sides equal.

4q. A shape made of three or more straight lines is called a

4r. A shape with five sides is a

4s. A 50p coin is this shape.

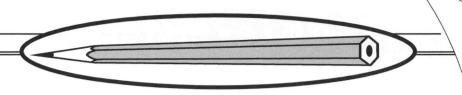

4t. Bees build with this shape. ☐

4w. A shape connected with US defence. ☐

4u. A figure with eight sides is an ☐

4x. A shape often used in making pencils. ☐

4v. A shape connected with a sea-creature. ☐

3-D shapes

5a. How many faces does a cube have? _ _ _ _ _ _ _

5b. What shape is each face on a cube? _ _ _ _ _ _ _

5c. A cylinder is a circular _ _ _ _ _ _ _

Symmetry

5d. How many lines of symmetry does a rectangle have? _ _ _ _ _ _ _

5e. The order of rotation of a square is _ _ _ _ _ _ _

5f. The order of rotation of a regular pentagon is _ _ _ _ _ _ _

Measures

5g. 4km = ☐ m

5l. 1.625kg = ☐ g

5h. 3m = ☐ cm

5m. 1 hour = ☐ seconds

5j. 5l = ☐ ml

5n. 1 leap year = ☐ days

5k. 2.5kg = ☐ g

5o. 1 millennium = ☐ years

Mark your score out of 122:

_____

122

If you have got all the questions correct, colour in this star.

glossary of terms

Analogue Analogue clocks and watches have hands that move round a face. They work on a 12-hour system, where *a.m.* means before midday and *p.m.* means after midday.

Arc An arc is any part of the circumference of a circle.

Area Area is the space occupied by 2-dimensional figures such as squares, triangles and circles.

Average To find the average of a group of numbers we add all the numbers together and divide the answer by the number of numbers.

Bar Chart A bar chart is a diagram showing information in a way that is easy to understand. A bar chart looks like several blocks of flats standing near each other.

Capacity Capacity is a measure normally used for liquids such as petrol and milk.

Chord A chord is a straight line joining any 2 points on the circumference of a circle.

Circumference The circumference is the line marking the outside of a circle.

Concentric circles Concentric circles are 2 or more circles with the same centre.

Cone A cone is a circular pyramid in which the cross sections gradually diminish to a point.

Cube A cube is a 3-dimensional shape with 6 identical square faces.

Cube number A cube number is the result you obtain when you multiply a number by itself and then multiply this answer once more by the original number. Thus the cube of 3 = 3 x 3 x 3 = 27. This can be written as 3^3.

Cuboid A Cuboid is a 3-dimensional shape with 6 rectangle faces. A brick is a good example.

Cylinder A cylinder is circular prism. Any slice of it is a circle. A good example is a Swiss roll.

Decimal A decimal indicates a part of something. Its written form uses a decimal point. Thus 0.1 indicates 1 tenth.

Denominator A denominator is the bottom number in a fraction. Thus in $\frac{3}{4}$ the denominator is 4. The top number is the numerator. The Lowest Common Denominator (LCD) is the lowest number that 2 or more denominators divide into exactly.

Diameter The diameter is any straight line going right across a circle and passing through the centre of the circle.

Equilateral Triangle An equilateral triangle has 3 equal sides and 3 equal angles. Each angle is 60°.

Factor A factor is a number that divides exactly into another number.

Fraction A fraction is a part of something. The most common fraction is a half, written as $\frac{1}{2}$.

Heptagon A heptagon is a 7-sided 2-dimensional figure. A 50p coin is in the shape of a heptagon.

Hexagon A hexagon is a 6-sided 2-dimensional figure.

Isosceles An isosceles triangle has 2 sides of equal length and 2 equal angles.

Kite A kite is a quadrilateral having 2 equal sides that touch each other and 2 longer sides of equal length that also touch each other.

Line Graph A line graph is a diagram that presents information through the rise and fall of a line.

Line of Symmetry A line of symmetry cuts a shape into 2 exact halves, so that if the paper is folded along the line of symmetry the 2 halves will coincide exactly.

Mean The mean is often called the 'average.' To find the mean of a group of numbers, we add all the numbers together and divide the answer by the number of numbers.

Median The median is the number that comes in the middle when a group of numbers is written out in order of size.

Mixed Number A mixed number consists of a whole number and a fraction. Examples are $1\frac{1}{2}$ and $2\frac{3}{4}$.

Mode The mode is the number which occurs most often in a group of numbers.

Multiple A multiple is the result of multiplying one number by another. Some multiples of 4 are 8, 12, 16, 24, 28.

Negative Numbers Negative numbers have a value less than zero. They are written with a minus sign in front of them, such as –2.

Numerator A numerator is the top number in a fraction. Thus in $\frac{3}{4}$ the numerator is 3. The bottom number is the denominator.

Octagon An octagon is an 8-sided 2-dimensional figure.

Order of Rotation The order of rotation is the number of times a shape, when turned, fits exactly into its original outline. Thus a square has an order of rotation of 4.

Parallelogram A parallelogram is a quadrilateral with 2 pairs of parallel sides. Its opposite angles are equal.

Pentagon A pentagon is a 5-sided 2-dimensional figure.

Percentage A percentage tells us how many parts there are out of 100. Thus 3% means 3 parts out of 100.

Pie Chart A pie chart is a circular diagram which presents information in a way that is easy to understand.

Place Value Place value is the value of a digit according to its place in a number. In 104 the digit 1 has a value of 100, but in 215 the digit 1 has a value of 10.

Polygon A polygon is a 2-dimensional shape made of 3 or more straight sides.

Prime Number A prime number has only 2 factors: 1 and the number itself. A prime factor is a prime number that divides exactly into another number.

Probability Probability is the likelihood of something happening.

Quadrilateral A quadrilateral is a 4-sided, 2-dimensional figure.

Radius The radius of a circle is any straight line from the centre of the circle to the circumference.

Rectangle A rectangle is a quadrilateral with 4 right angles.

Reflective Symmetry Reflective symmetry refers to a shape where 2 halves are perfect mirror images of each other.

Rhombus A rhombus is a parallelogram which has all its sides the same length. It helps to think of it as a diamond.

Rotational Symmetry Rotational symmetry refers to a shape which, when turned, fits its original outline exactly.

Rounding Rounding means expressing a number approximately rather than precisely.

Scalene A scalene triangle has no equal sides and therefore has no equal angles.

Sector A sector of a circle is like a slice of pizza. It has 2 straight edges, which are radii, and a curved side, which is an arc.

Segment A segment is a slice of a circle. It has 1 straight edge, which is a chord, and 1 curved edge, which is an arc.

Semi-circle A semi-circle is half a circle.

Square Number A square number is the answer you obtain when you multiply any number by itself. Thus the square of 3 = 3 x 3 = 9, which is written as $3.^2$

Symmetry *See Line of Symmetry, Reflective Symmetry, Rotational Symmetry.*

Tessellation Tessellation is a pattern made of shapes that fit snugly together.

Tiling Tiling is a tessellation pattern made of a single repeating shape.

Top Heavy Fraction This is often called an *improper fraction*. Its numerator is larger than its denominator. Examples are $\frac{11}{9}$ and $\frac{3}{2}$.

Trapezium A trapezium is a quadrilateral with a single pair of parallel lines.

Triangle A triangle is a 3-sided 2-dimensional figure.

Multiplication Table

1	2	3	4	5	6	7	8	9	10	11	12	13	14	15	16	17	18	19	20
2	4	6	8	10	12	14	16	18	20	22	24	26	28	30	32	34	36	38	40
3	6	9	12	15	18	21	24	27	30	33	36	39	42	45	48	51	54	57	60
4	8	12	16	20	24	28	32	36	40	44	48	52	56	60	64	68	72	76	80
5	10	15	20	25	30	35	40	45	50	55	60	65	70	75	80	85	90	95	100
6	12	18	24	30	36	42	48	54	60	66	72	78	84	90	96	102	108	114	120
7	14	21	28	35	42	49	56	63	70	77	84	91	98	105	112	119	126	133	140
8	16	24	32	40	48	56	64	72	80	88	96	104	112	120	128	136	144	152	160
9	18	27	36	45	54	63	72	81	90	99	108	117	126	135	144	153	162	171	180
10	20	30	40	50	60	70	80	90	100	110	120	130	140	150	160	170	180	190	200
11	22	33	44	55	66	77	88	99	110	121	132	143	154	165	176	187	198	209	220
12	24	36	48	60	72	84	96	108	120	132	144	156	168	180	192	204	216	228	240
13	26	39	52	65	78	91	104	117	130	143	156	169	182	195	208	221	234	247	260
14	28	42	56	70	84	98	112	126	140	154	168	182	196	210	224	238	252	266	280
15	30	45	60	75	90	105	120	135	150	165	180	195	210	225	240	255	270	285	300
16	32	48	64	80	96	112	128	144	160	176	192	208	224	240	256	272	288	304	320
17	34	51	68	85	102	119	136	153	170	187	204	221	238	255	272	289	306	323	340
18	36	54	72	90	108	126	144	162	180	198	216	234	252	270	288	306	324	342	360
19	38	57	76	95	114	133	152	171	190	209	228	247	266	285	304	323	342	361	380
20	40	60	80	100	120	140	160	180	200	220	240	260	280	300	320	340	360	380	400

Answers

Answers

Test 1
a. 200, 5, **b.** 2,000, 50, **c.** 2, 500, **d.** 20,00, 5,000, **e.** 20, 50,000, **f.** 10,000, 400, **g.** 10, 4000, **h.** 1, 40, **i.** 100, 4, **j.** 30, **k.** 80, **l.** 100, **m.** 300, **n.** 4,000, **o.** 20, **p.** 30, **q.** 300, **r.** 6,000, **s.** 70

Test 2
a. 866, **b.** 2352, **c.** 2494, **d.** 0 **e.** 32 **f.** 811 **g.** 438 **h.** 208 **i.** 267 **j.** £5.82 **k.** 275m **l.** 223

Test 3
a. 3,024, **b.** 6,984, **c.** 3,770, **d.** 4,004, **e.** 5,890, **f.** 8,428, **g.** 2,373, **h.** 6,048, **i.** 3,870, **j.** 390 **k.** 306

Test 4
a. 24 r4, **b.** 61 r1, **c.** 66 r11, **d.** 446 r12, **e.** 577 r11, **f.** 111 r9, **g.** 203, **h.** 305r2, **i.** 200, **j.** 79r4, **k.** £1838,

Test 5
a. 18 24 30 36 42, **b.** 21 28 35 42 49, **c.** 24 32 40 48 56, **d.** 27 36 45 54 63, **e.** 36 48 60 72 84, **f.** 1 2 3 6, **g.** 1 2 4 8 **h.** 1 2 4 8 16, **i.** 1 2 4 5 10 20, **j.** 1 2 3 5 6 10 15 30, **k.** 5 7 11 13 17, **l.** 2 3, **m.** 2 3 5,

Test 6
a. 1/2, **b.** 1/3, **c.** 1/4, **d.** 1/3, **e.** 2/4 = 1/2, **f.** 3/5, **g.** 1/6, **h.** 3\8, **i.** 7/10, **j.** 2/3, **k.** 1/2, **l.** 1/3, **m.** 1/2, **n.** 1/2, **o.** 1/4, **p.** 1/3, **q.** 1/5, **r.** 1/2, **s.** 2/5, **t.** 3/5 **u.** 4/5, **v.** 1/6, **w.** 1/4, **x.** 1/3 **y.** 2/3, **z.** 3/4.

Test 7
a. 5/9, **b.** 4/5, **c.** 2/3, **d.** 6/7, **e.** 7/8, **f.** 7/10, **g.** 4/9, **h.** 10/11, **i.** 11/12, **j.** 3/5, **k.** 1/3, **l.** 3/7, **m.** 4/11, **n.** 7/17, **o.** 12/23, **p.** 5/19, **q.** 8/21, **r.** 2/15, **s.** 4 3 7, **t.** 5 4 9 **u.** 2/4 + 1/4 = 3/4, **v.** 3/10 + 2/10 = 5/10 = 1/2, **w.** 2/6 + 1/6 = 3/6 = 1/2, **x.** 7/21 + 3/21 = 10/21, **y.** 4/18 - 3/18 = 1/18, **z.** 15/18 - 3/18 = 12/18 = 2/3. **aa.** 6/8 - 5/8 = 1/8, **bb.** 15/21 - 6/21 = 9/21 = 3/7

Test 8
a. 2/27, **b.** 3/50, **c.** 1/6, **d.** 1/4, **e.** 1/8, **f.** 1/16, **g.** 2/15, **h.** 3/14, **i.** 1/4, **j.** 1/6, **k.** 4/11, **l.** 7/12, **m.** 1 1/4, **n.** 1 4/5, **o.** 1 1/2 **p.** 1 2/9, **q.** 1 6/7, **r.** 2 3/6 = 2 1/2, **s.** 1/8 x 3/2 = 3/16, **t.** 2/7 x 5/3 = 10/21, **u.** 4/9 x 3/1 = 12/9 = 1 3/9 = 1 1/3, **v.** 3/4 x 8/1 = 6, **w.** 3/8 x 3/2 = 9/16, **x.** 4/5 x 15/2 = 2/1 x 3/1 = 6 **y.** 2/9 x 9/3 = 2/1 x 1/3 = 2/3, **z.** 5/11 x 33/10 = 1/1 x 3/2 = 3/2 = 1 1/2, **aa.** 1/4 x 2/1 = 1/2 x 1/1 = 1/2, **bb.** 1/3 x 6/1 = 1/1 x 2/1 = 2 **cc.** 1/6 x 3/1 = 1/2 x 1/1 = 1/2 **dd.** 7/10 x 5/1 = 7/2 x 1/1 = 7/2 = 3 1/2

Test 9
a. 1.03, **b.** 0.809, **c.** 4.689, **d.** 49.119, **e.** 24.96, **f.** 1.302, **g.** 2.519, **h.** 0.027, **i.** 7.47, **j.** 4.124, **k.** 0.912, **l.** 5.714, **m.** 0.73, **n.** 0.45, **o.** 0.168, **p.** 0.4688, **q.** 0.71, **r.** 0.32, **s.** 0.125 **t.** 1.037, **u.** 0.31, **v.** 1.05, **w.** 0.122, **x.** 0.016

Test 10
a. 7, **b.** 6.8, **c.** 12.5, **d.** 0.1, **e.** 42.8, **f.** 30, **g.** 650.2, **h.** 0.2, **i.** 0.07, **j.** 0.005, **k.** 0.12, **l.** 2.467, **m.** 0.1676, **n.** 0.0265, **o.** 1.798, **p.** 37.9401

Test 11
a. £5, **b.** £30, **c.** £40, **d.** 8p, **e.** 5m, **f.** £100, **g.** £2.25, **h.** 50%, **i.** 90%, **j.** 95%.

Test 12
a. 16 32 64 128 256 512 1024, **b.** 50, **c.** 70, **d.** 90, **e.** £3, **f.** £4.50, **g.** £2.30, **h.** 300, **i.** 900, **j.** 1300 **k.** 150, **l.** 350, **m.** 550, **n.** 5.0, **o.** 19.0, **p.** 25.0, **q.** 10mm or 1cm, **r.** 1000m or 1km, **s.** 1500g, **t.** 300 150 75, **u.** £4, **v.** £3.50, **w.** £7.50, **x.** 25 **y.** 35, **z.** 45, **aa.** 1,000,000, **bb.** 500,000, **cc.** 1/2kg or 500g, **dd.** 49m, **ee.** 1.6, **ff.** 1,350.

Test 13
a. 1, **b.** 4, **c.** 9, **d.** 16, **e.** 25, **f.** 36, **g.** 49, **h.** 64, **i.** 81 **j.** 100, **k.** 121, **l.** 144, **m.** 1, **n.** 8, **o.** 27, **p.** 64, **q.** 125, **r.** 216, **s.** 343, **t.** 512, **u.** 729, **v.** 1,000, **w.** 4, **x.** 5, **y.** 12, **z.** 17, **aa.** 7, **bb.** 4, **cc.** 3, **dd.** 24, **ee.** 2, **ff.** 12.

Test 14
a. 2, **b.** 3, **c.** 4, **d.** 2, **e.** 3, **f.** 4, **g.** 5, **h.** 6, **i.** 7, **j.** 8, **k.** 9, **l.** 10, **m.** 2, **n.** 3, **o.** 4, **p.** 2, **q.** 3, **r.** 4, **s.** 3, **t.** 4, **u.** 5.

Test 15
a. Summer **b.** £4,000 **c.** £1,000, **d.** June, July, August, September, **e.** January, December, **f.** It's too cold to enjoy ice-cream, **g.** People enjoy ice-cream in warm weather, **h.** £5,000, **i.** February, March

Test 16
a.

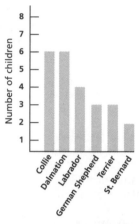

b. Collies and Dalmations, **c.** St. Bernards, **d.** 4.

Test 17
a. 6, **b.** Yes, **c.** 1, **d.** The rainy slice is much bigger than the sunny slice, **e.** Sunny and icy, **f.** 1.

Test 18
a. 1/4, **b.** 1/13, **c.** 2/13, **d.** 1/2, **e.** 1/2, **f.** 1/2, **g.** 1/6, **h.** 1/2, **i.** 1/2, **j.** 1/2, **k.** 1/6,

Test 19
a. 18, **b.** 12, **c.** 12, **d.** 10, **e.** 6, **f.** 8, **g.** 5, **h.** 6, **i.** 5, **j.** £3, **k.** 137cm.

Test 20
a. 4cm, **b.** 1.5cm, **c.** 12cm, **d.** 5cm, **e.** 7cm, **f.** 1.25cm, **g.** 0.5cm, **h.** 4.5cm, **i.** 3cm, **j.** 2.8cm **k.** 2cm, **l.** 10.2cm, **m.** 6.28cm, **n.** 12.56cm, **o.** 18.84cm, **p.** 25.12cm, **q.** 3.14cm, **r.** 9.42cm, **s.** 15.7cm, **t.** 21.98cm, **u.** $3.14cm^2$, **v.** $12.56cm^2$, **w.** $28.26cm^2$, **x.** $50.24cm^2$, **y.** $78.5cm^2$, **z.** $113.04cm^2$.

Test 21

a.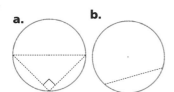
b.

c.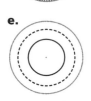
d.

e.

Test 22
a. equilateral,
b. scalene,
c. right-angled,
d. isosceles

Test 23
a. $x = 80°$, b. $x = 60°$,
c. $x = 70°$,$y = 40°$,
d. $x = 65°$ $y = 65°$,
e. $x = 70°$, f. $x = 60°$,
g. $x = 20°$

Test 24
a. $12cm^2$, b. $14cm^2$,
c. $20cm^2$, d. $9cm^2$,
e. $24cm^2$, f. $12cm^2$.

Test 25
a. trapezium
b. rectangle
c. kite, d. parallelogram,
e. rhombus,
f. square,
g. parallelogram,
h. trapezium, i. square,
j. kite, k. rhombus,
l. rectangle.

Test 26
a. triangle, b. square,
c. heptagon, d. pentagon,
e. hexagon, f. octagon,
g. heptagon, h. hexagon,
i. pentagon, j. hexagon,
k. octagon.

Test 27
a. three-dimensional,
b. 6, c. square,
d. rectangle, e. 12,
f. cylinder, g. cuboid,
h. 5, i. 5,
j.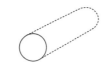

k.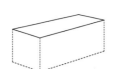

l.

m.

n.

o.

Test 28
a. 4,
b.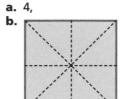

c. 6,
d.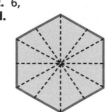

e.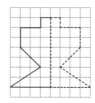

f.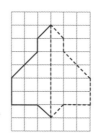

g. 2, h. 3, i. 6

Test 29
a.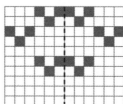

b.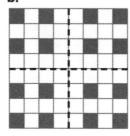

c.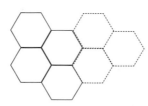

Test 30
a. kilometre, b. metre,
c. metre, d. metre,
e. centimetre,
f. millimetre,
g. millimetre, h. 3,000,
i. 200, j. 25, k. 4,500,
l. 625, m. 26, n. 3.5,
o. 1.5, p. 1.25, q. 35,

r. 7.48, s. 10.672,
t. 300, u. 1,000, v. 420,
w. 3.6, x. 8,620,
y. 2,100, z. 50.

Test 31
a. kilogram, b. tonne,
c. gramme,
d. milligrammes,
e. 1,500, f. 0.25, g. 1.3,
h. 1,500, i. 350, j. 1.2,
k. 3,500, l. 2,000, m. 50,
n. 0.3, o. litre, p. litre,
q. millilitre, r. 2,000,
s. 200, t. 0.5, u. 70,
v. 80, w. 4.5, x. 5,000
y. 30

Test 32
a. weeks, b. seconds,
c. years, d. weeks,
e. decades, f. centuries,
g. millenium, h. 35mins,
i. 1hr 20mins,
j. October 3rd,
k. 5:05 p.m., l. 7:50,
m. 4:48 p.m., n. 20:27,
o. 1:01 p.m., p. 18:05,
q. 11:59 p.m.

Revision Practice
a. 70, b. 40, c. 40,
d. 500, e. 2,284, f. 563,
g. 578, h. 26,296,
i. 1,800 j. 165r12,
k. 306r7, l. £200,
m. 200, n. 52 65 78,
o. 1 2 3 6 9 18,
p. 1 5 7 35.

Page 71
q. 11, r. false, s. 2 3,
t. true, u. true, v. 1/4
1/3 1/2, w. part of
something,
x. half, y. 0.1 z. 0.01,
aa. 1%, bb. numerator,
cc. denominator, dd. 0.5,
ee. 50%, ff. 75%.
gg. 4/9, hh. 5/7, ii. 5/6,
jj. 1/6, kk. 1/20, ll. 1/5,
mm. 2/3, nn. 4/9,
oo. 1 1/4, pp. 0.74,
qq. 1.202, rr. 0.156,
ss. 6.25, tt. 62.5,
uu. 0.0625, vv. 0.00625.
ww. £3, xx. 50p,
yy. £1.50 zz. 150,
ab. 10mm, ac. 1.6,
ad. 4, ae. 25, af. 6,
ag. 27, ah. 5,

Page 72: Handling Data
a. kiwis, **b.** bananas,
c. 9, **d.** satsumas, **e.** 3,
f. grapes , **g.** bananas,
h.

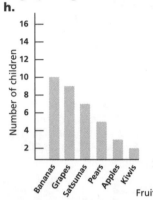

Page 73: Geometry
2i. 6, **2j.** 6, **2k.** 6,
2l. 62%, **3a.** circumference,
3b. radius, **3c.** diameter,
3d. semi-circle, **3e.** 2πr
3f. πr², **3g.** Greek,
3h. 2.4cm, **3i.** 2.45cm,
3j. 90º, **3k.** chord, **3l.** 2,
3m. concentric,

Page 74: Triangles,
Quadralaterals, Polyons,
4a. 3, **4b.** 180º,
4c. right-angled,
4d. equilateral, **4e.** 60º,
4f. isoscoles, **4g.** scalene,
4h. angles, **4i.** 63º,
4j. 12cm², **4k.** 4, **4l.** 2,
4m. trapezium,
4n. rhombus,
4o. rectangle/square,
4p. square, **4q.** polygon,
4r. pentagon,
4s. heptagon.

Page 75
4t. hexagon,
4u. octagon,
4v. octagon,
4w. pentagon,
4x. hexagon,

5a. 6, **5b.** square
5c. prism, **5d.** 2, **5e.** 4,
5f. 5, **5g.** 4,000,
5h. 300, **5j.** 5,000,
5k. 2,500, **5l.** 1,625,
5m. 3,600, **5n.** 366,
5o. 1,000,